GRAVE
Bruce Highway

By Helen Goltz & Chris Adams

Atlas Productions

This book is supported by the Queensland Government through Arts Queensland.

Queensland
Government

GRAVE TALES: BRUCE HIGHWAY

Publisher: Atlas Productions
Greenslopes QLD 4102
Web: www.atlasproductions.com.au

Authors' note: We have taken great care to be respectful to the people featured in *Grave Tales* – in the telling of their life stories, and to any living descendants. Our intent is to save our history and share the tales of the many lives that have gone before us. **Please note:** where errors have appeared in quotes and newsclippings, we have left them as they were originally written or intended.

Cover images (please see individual chapters for full source details). Top row, left to right: Sgt. Henry Buchanan, kindly supplied by Sgt. Buchanan's great nephew, Damon Bickle; Emma Watson, courtesy of State Library of Queensland; Thomas Griffin, courtesy of State Libary of Queensland; José Paronella, kindly supplied by the Evans family of Paronella Park; Jack Miles, kindly supplied by Australia @ War. Bottom row, left to right: Nurse Cecelia Bauer, kindly supplied by the Wide Bay Hospitals Museum Inc.; James Nash, courtesy of State Library of Queensland; Dorinda Curtis (nee Parker), kindly supplied by the Central Queensland University Library; Inigo Jones, courtesy of State Library of Queensland; Sarah Welch, kindly supplied by Cathy Head and the Welch family descendants.
Cemetery image: West End Cemetery, Townsville photo by Heritage branch staff [Public domain], via Wikimedia Commons.

A catalogue record for this book is available from the National Library of Australia

NATIONAL LIBRARY OF AUSTRALIA

*"If history were taught in the form of stories,
it would never be forgotten."*

Rudyard Kipling

Contents by cemetery:

Contents by story:

Donation:

We are proud to donate $1 from the sale of every *Grave Tales: Bruce Highway* paperback to providing gravestones or restoring damaged gravestones for the people we feature in our *Grave Tales* series.

Introduction

I suppose it's not a bad way to start out... being named after a politician who they reckoned was a 'good bloke'. I speak of Harry Bruce who was the state minister in charge of Queensland roads and the like in the mid-1930s... although, despite the calls from those who say the road is neglected, I venture to say that there would hardly be a metre of the roadway that Harry would recognise these days.

Harry was given the honour because, essentially, he got the thing happening. It was originally designated as a 'tourist road' and named the 'Great North Road' which in reality was just a fancy name for a gravel track that ran from somewhere in behind the Redcliffe peninsula to Eumundi – still it was stage one of the Bruce Highway.

In a relatively short time the road has evolved from a terrible old dirt track to a modern highway. I'm not saying it doesn't constantly need work and improving... like all roads with increasing volumes of traffic and the changing nature of transport... it always will.

In the 1950s, I remember my grandparents setting off in the dickie-seat equipped Dodge to drive from Melbourne to Mackay and return. Fair dinkum, you'd think they were travelling to the moon and back. I remember as a kid seeing some of their photos; the road wasn't sealed... in places it looked like two sets of tyre tracks running parallel through jungle, and in other places, dust... dust so dense you couldn't see 20 feet.

Even when I first drove the highway on my way north to Townsville in 1970 it was little better than a goat track. I was travelling to take up my first full-time job in radio and spent most of the drive wondering if this was what the roads were like, what would the radio station be like? I remember steep inclines down to creek beds where the bridges were little better than fords... then up the corrugated climb on the other side. Great herds of cattle that materialised in the middle of the road as you came around a bend. There were potholes you could hide a truck in... I was lucky to get there.

But I had it easy when you read some of the stories of the people who came to this part of the world in the early days. The Gympie miners who battled their way over a rough track so bad that many went to Maryborough by steamer and walked to Gympie from there. Miners on the Palmer goldfields of north Queensland... again they walked from Cooktown in the heat and humidity.

And what about Christie Palmerston, who marked out the tracks around Cairns and Port Douglas and Innisfail. He and his party walked the journey from Mourilyan Harbour to Herberton... about 100 kilometres in 12 days... and that was considered to be 'express'!

So now this road we call the Bruce Highway first passes

through the expanses of the Sunshine Coast, on to Gympie and Maryborough, and then to Rockhampton... to Mackay and north to Townsville and Cairns... and we've tacked a little bit on the end to tell the Mary Watson story from Cooktown. These are all places where great stories lie – tales of ordinary people caught up in extraordinary events. *Grave Tales* – enjoy.

Chris Adams

Above: Along the Bruce Highway 1958. A Ford Prefect on the road between Brisbane and Cairns. Photo: courtesy of Mrs Woolley and the State Library of Queensland.

Reference:
Woolley, Leslie Albert, Woolley Collection of Slides, Ford Prefect on the road between Brisbane and Cairns, Queensland, 1958. *John Oxley Library, State Library of Queensland.* Reprinted with the kind permission of Mrs Woolley. Accession number: 6668. Retrieved 17 August 2017 via URL: http://hdl.handle.net/10462/comp/343.

The man for all seasons
Inigo Jones

Interred: Inigo Owen Jones, 1 December 1872 – 14 November 1954 (aged 82 years).

Location: Front row, Peachester Cemetery.

Cemetery: Peachester Cemetery, Cemetery Road, Crohamhurst, QLD 4519.

Hanrahan, the central figure of the Monsignor Patrick Joseph Hartigan poem, just a small part of which is reproduced here, was clearly the ultimate pessimist:

> *"If we don't get three inches, man,*
> *Or four to break this drought,*
> *We'll all be rooned," said Hanrahan,*
> *"Before the year is out."*
>
> *It pelted, pelted all day long,*
> *A-singing at its work,*
> *Till every heart took up the song*
> *Way out to Back-o'Bourke.*
>
> *And every creek a banker ran,*
> *And dams filled overtop;*
> *"We'll all be rooned," said Hanrahan,*
> *"If this rain doesn't stop."*[1]

No weather event could bring any good… it was all out to get him, to see his ruination. But Hanrahan had good reason for his pessimism, the fortunes of this nation have been dictated by our weather and it is still probably the most discussed topic on any day, in any town or suburb around Australia.

We have storms, hail and cyclones, droughts, floods, bushfires, dust storms, freezes and southerly busters or cool changes—depending on where you live—locust plagues and even tsunamis, although they have only rarely caused damage.

These are the dramatic faces of weather… the sharp end

that we all feel at one time or another, some with more drastic results than others. Since 1851 more than 800 people have died in Australian bushfires and over twenty thousand homes and other buildings destroyed or badly damaged. Countless millions of livestock and wildlife have perished and millions of hectares of farming land made useless... its fences, watering systems and stock feed destroyed. Then add the bridges, power lines, telephone towers, machinery in sheds, timber from plantations and the cost is quite simply... enormous.[2]

And there are also fatalities from extreme heat which caused 4500 deaths between 1900 and 2011.[3]

But most damage has been caused by drought, severe storms, hail and cyclones, perhaps because they commonly occur in more populated areas. A report from the Australian Business Roundtable for Disaster Resilience & Safer Communities found that over the ten years to 2016 the total cost of natural disasters to Australia averaged 18.2 billion dollars a year. It also shows that more than nine million Australians have been impacted by a natural disaster or extreme weather event over the last 30 years.[4]

So maybe there is a part of an annual bill of $18,200,000,000 that we might have saved... and some of the 9,000,000 people might not have been traumatised if we knew what the weather was going to do... and when. And 'they' tell us it is only going to get worse – the cost of natural disaster is predicted to reach 39 billion dollars a year by 2050.[5]

The idea of long-term prediction of what the weather will do is not new... far from it. And it's not new to Australia either.

Inigo looking at weather charts c1945-51. Source: State Library of Victoria.

Meet Inigo Jones

Enter a man called Inigo Owen Jones who arrived in Queensland with his parents in 1874 from Surrey in England. They lived in Kangaroo Point and young Inigo won a scholarship to attend Brisbane Grammar School. He was a keen student—of the stars and the atmosphere—and had an observatory in his parents' house.

So keen and knowledgeable was he that in 1888 the colonial meteorologist, a fellow by the name of Clement Wragge, a character in his own right, took him onboard as a cadet in his office… and young Jones learned from Wragge for the next five years. Wragge had originally set up his own private observatory near Adelaide but was invited to Queensland by the government after his suggestions as to how the number of ships lost to cyclones could be reduced.

He became well known in the colony and when, shortly after his arrival, the town received a deluge—18 inches (457mm) of rain in three weeks—the locals dubbed him 'Inclement' Wragge.

Wragge had an inquiring mind and wasn't tied down by conventional thinking… he was prepared to experiment… a trait which no doubt encouraged Inigo Jones to investigate non-traditional concepts. When the experienced Wragge started exploring the ideas of Edouard Bruckner, the German meteorologist and professor, Jones began to take notice. Bruckner investigated what appeared to be interchanging cold, wet periods with hot, dry ones in Europe's north-west.

The 35-year rotations became known as 'Bruckner Cycles' and the scientist investigated climate change and glacial climatology seeking an answer as to why it happened.

Inigo the predictor

At this point, Inigo Jones began to compare the 35-year changes, the basis of Bruckner's work, with the 11-year sunspot phases and took a keen interest in developing long-range forecasting on the basis of sunspots.

Put simply, he believed that droughts and floods in Queensland were caused by sunspots brought about by the interaction of the four major planets, Jupiter, Saturn, Uranus and Neptune. In his paper, *Inigo Jones: The Weather Prophet*, Tim Sherratt wrote:

> *"If you wanted to know what the weather would be like on 1 January next year, you would calculate the positions of the planets on that day and then look back through the record of weather observations to a time when the planetary positions were the same. If the locations of the planets matched, then so would the weather – more or less. Or perhaps less than more, for what seemed to set Jones apart from other weather prophets were the levels of complexity he added to this basic cyclical system."*[6]

According to author, David Burton, writing in *Your Trading Edge* magazine: "Inigo used these cycles and the Bruckner cycle of 35-36 years to predict the 1974 floods, which was 20 years after his death. He also predicted the great drought of 1983 to 1993, which was 30 years after his death."[7] And if there ever was a message from the weather gods for the emerging meteorologist, Inigo Jones, it came not long after his parents moved to a property they had bought on the Sunshine Coast hinterland and christened 'Crohamhurst', after a country estate near where Inigo was born in England.

Inigo joined them there with the intention of working the farm with his father and continuing his study of the weather, sunspots and long-range forecasting as a hobby. But soon after his arrival on 3 February 1893, he recorded an Australian record for the most rain in one day when 35.7 inches (907mm) fell in one 24-hour period.[8] It's a record that still stands.

The rain came on the back of Cyclone Buninyong which also brought devastating floods to Brisbane and Ipswich; 35 people died including seven miners who were drowned at the Eclipse Colliery in North Ipswich. The Albert Railway bridge at Indooroopilly and the northern end of the Victoria Bridge were washed away and two ships including the gunboat *Paluma* were carried into the Botanic Gardens. The city was devastated and felt the effect of the Great 1893 Flood for years to come.

It was a classic example where information on what we might expect weather-wise, long-range forecasting, could have saved lives and allowed Brisbane and Ipswich residents to be better prepared. And Inigo was to experience the 'man on the land's' dependence on weather forecasts while he lived a fairly private life as Farmer Jones for almost the next 30 years.

Life on the farm

In 1905 he married a young lady from Brisbane, Marion Emma Comrie, and they lived on the property which would eventually become the headquarters of Inigo's long-range forecasting business. Inigo and Marion had three daughters and one son. Life wasn't always kind to them… their son, Meredith, died while still an infant in May 1914.

Toward the end of 1923, Queensland was in dire straits during a drought that had created havoc in rural areas, including scenes hard to imagine in the north of the state, as noted in *The Register*:

"Cairns advisers state that the continued dry weather is causing the gravest anxiety throughout the whole far north. Bush fires are raging in all districts and are burning sugar fields in their onward sweep... The famed Barron Falls are reduced to a trickle... So serious is the shortage in the Innisfail area that hotels and private places are forced to obtain water at considerable cost. Not before in the history of the district has such a serious drought been experienced."[9]

It took a brave man to predict that this misery being felt across the state of Queensland was about to end... but Inigo, based on his sunspot readings, did just that. And when the 'big dry' did end, the publicity that surrounded Inigo Jones made him a household name. People wanted his forecasts... so much so that by 1935 he set up the Crohamhurst Observatory at his family farm.

In demand

And the Queensland Government wanted him, appointing him director of the Bureau of Seasonal Forecasting of the Council of Agriculture. Farmers wanted to know about the man who could predict when droughts would come and go... but ironically, it was another accurate prediction of a change in the weather when the nation was sweltering that brought about what was probably the harshest scientific criticism he encountered in his 60 or more years of observations.

It happened in January 1939 while the greatest scientific minds of this country and some eminent visitors from overseas, including science-fiction writer, HG Wells, were meeting at the Australian and New Zealand Association for the Advancement of Science (ANZAAS) in Canberra.

The country was at that time in the grip of a heat wave which would kill over four hundred people and culminate in the disastrous Black Friday bushfires of 13 January. Earlier in the week as the 800 delegates to the conference gathered in the nation's capital, the temperature had regularly been topping the 100 degrees Fahrenheit mark (37.8 degrees Celsius). On the opening day of the conference, it was no different... the temperature quickly rose to a Canberra record 108.5F (42.5C).

Amongst the reports of temperatures as high as 122F (50C) across the land, bushfires, deaths by heat exhaustion and buckled railway lines, *The Canberra Times* featured a story headlined "INIGO JONES FORECASTS RAIN TODAY". In the body of the copy it reported: "Most interest of a scientific character centred in a courageous prophecy by Mr Inigo Jones the famous Queensland weather forecaster, that by to-day it would be cool and raining in Canberra. Mr. Inigo Jones was quite confident in his prediction." [10]

And it did rain... well sort of. *The Canberra Times* again: "It seemed that Mr. Inigo Jones had won out shortly before 4pm when the wind changed suddenly to a cool westerly and brought a brief rainstorm which sent guests at the garden party at Parliament House scurrying for shelter. When the wind and rain passed, conditions were more unpleasant than ever. The atmosphere was heavy and muggy."[11]

Jones' presentation at the conference was almost overshadowed by the weather events, but essentially, he said that: "After fifty years' study he remained convinced that these cycles held the 'key to the puzzle' of seasonal forecasting."[12] But it wasn't a view held by all of those who heard his presentation and when the New Zealand government meteorologist, Edward Kidson, rose to comment he said that any detailed analysis of Inigo Jones' paper would be a waste of time. He dismissed him by saying that Jones had no clear mental picture of the mechanisms he was describing and the paper: "...fell far below the standard which should be expected in a communication to such a gathering of scientists."[13] Inigo took it all fairly philosophically saying: "They ridiculed Galileo, too in his day." [14]

Long-range weather forecaster, Inigo Jones, with Bernard Henry Corser at the opening of the Crohamhurst Observatory, ca. 1935, State Library of Qld.

A loyal following

'The bush' was outraged… with a farmer's views expressed in *The Land* editorial of Friday 20 January:

> *"To the man on the land, whose business depends on weather conditions and to whom rain becomes a dominating factor in his year's work, there will be little interest in scientific squabbles and jealousies. For long range weather forecasting the farmer wants results. Those results have been given him by Mr Inigo Jones. Dr Kidson and his colleagues may object to the system but they cannot deny its undoubted success."* [15]

Despite Inigo's theories never being proved conclusively, he still had a very large following in Australia… particularly with the 'man on the land'. There was also curious interest from newspapers, with many publishers printing Inigo's long-range predictions every time there was a missive from Crohamhurst. In 1942, agricultural-based organisations put their money where their mouth was and, with a little help from the Queensland government, raised enough money to establish the Inigo Jones Seasonal Weather Forecasting Trust to finance the work at Crohamhurst.

Inigo was by now in his early seventies and his life-long study of the stars and planets, the sun and its effect on our planet and the rest of our galaxy had convinced him that there are certain principles at work that we may well take heed of today. He outlined his beliefs in a letter to a friend, Horace Flower, which was printed in *The Pastoral Review and Grazier's Record* of 16 December 1954, just a few weeks after Inigo's death in November of that year:

"You advocate co-operation. Now, if as I say, the whole universe is just a vast electro-magnetic machine of which our planets are part, and we individuals too are magnetic units, then Nature shows us that co-operation in living is the only way of life. If, in a magnetic machine, any part became more forcible than another, then the whole machine would be out of balance and go wrong with disastrous results."[16]

And that from a man who was for many years on the Synod of the Brisbane Diocese of the Anglican Church.

Inigo and Marion Jones in their garden at Crohamhurst with their dog [unnamed], ca 1935. Source: State Library of Qld.

An apprentice begins

About 18 months before he died, Inigo took on an apprentice, a 29-year-old ex-serviceman who had put his age forward and served on the Kokoda Trail at just sixteen-and-a-half. His name was Robert Lennox Walker... but everyone just called him Lennox. By now business was booming at Crohamhurst and Lennox recalled that one of his early tasks was to deal with inquiries by brides-to-be. Every day the mailbag brought about 20 letters from women all across the country wanting to know what the weather would be like for their 'big day'.

With the death of the 'great man' as the papers called him, Lennox would become the Research Director at the observatory and said his single ambition was to prove the theories developed by Inigo Jones.[17]

He also had one task to finish for Inigo... to issue his last forecast prepared for Christmas 1954. Inigo had wanted to send it out but was tired the day before his death and postponed it. The forecast said 'Fine and Hot from Brisbane to Adelaide... becoming more pleasant towards New Year's Day.'[18]

Was he right? It's a bit hard to tell from more than 60 years on, but a look at Christmas Day, December averages and New Year's Day 1955 temperatures tells us a little. The areas from Sydney south and the sweep around through Melbourne, the south west of Victoria and across to Adelaide had hotter Christmas Days than their December average, as Inigo predicted. Between Brisbane and Sydney it was a little cooler than the December average. On the other side of the coin, a random selection of towns and cities from

Brisbane around to Adelaide shows that, with Melbourne and Adelaide as the exceptions, all had a hotter New Year's Day than Christmas Day. [19]

But it was, and still probably is, an inexact science. In this particular case, call it 50/50. It's an interesting result given that a committee which investigated Inigo's methods and claims in the early 1950s came up with the same result.[20] But does that invalidate his work? Jones' biographer, Tim Sherratt, wrote:

"Even if Jones' predictions were not valid, he was providing farmers with data on average seasonal conditions in a form that they could use and understand. It may have been that not only the content of his forecasts was important, but the way landholders integrated them with their own knowledge of the local environment."[21]

Regardless of the committee's findings, the long-range forecasters from Crohamhurst still had a remarkable number of followers amongst farmers, who believed that even if the forecasts were not accurate to the day, they predicted the timing of trends so that farmers could manage the timing of events on their properties, like sowing and harvesting, stocking and selling off… without incurring massive losses.

Lennox Walker ran the enterprise for 41 years after Inigo's death. Crohamhurst passed from his control in 1993 and is now a private farm. It was added to the Queensland Heritage Register in 2008.

As well as his service to farmers Lennox still responded to wedding inquiries and people wanting to know if it would be fine for their holiday… and even punters asking him for a track report:

"A punter rang me some years ago hoping for a wet track for the Melbourne Cup. 'It will be', I told him. 'Then back Van Der Hum', he said. I did. It teemed, and Van Der Hum won. (It was 1976, one of the wettest and slowest cups on record.)" [22]

Another big tick for Lennox was his forecast for the 1956 Melbourne Olympic Games, which had plenty of doubters… but after a period of intense rain the fine weather he had predicted arrived.

At 68 years of age and after 41 years of forecasting Lennox Walker handed the business and the knowledge over to his son Hayden. Lennox died in 2000 and was cremated at Nambour. Hayden still runs the business but now operates from Bundaberg as fourth in a remarkable line of men—Wragge, Jones and the two Walkers—whose lifelong challenge has been to understand why weather does what it does.

When you visit Inigo, Marion and some of their family in Peachester cemetery you can travel just a couple of kilometres further and see part of the legacy he left us… of which his long-time friend and confidant, Horace Flower, wrote:

"A living memorial to Inigo grows upon about fifty acres (a bit over 20 hectares) of his original farm land which he gave to the Forestry Department to plant Pine forest upon it. These trees keep growing year by year within sight of the little Crohamhurst Observatory where the kindly visionary, Inigo Jones, kept vigil with the sun, moon and stars." [23]

How to find Inigo Jones's grave and Peachester Cemetery:

There are no graves easier to find than those of Inigo and his family. Once you have arrived at Peachester Cemetery, simply enter through the front shelter, turn left and the Jones' graves are right in front of you.

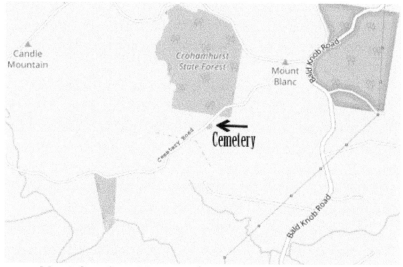

Map:©OpenStreetMap contributors. www.openstreetmap.org

Images:

Inigo Jones between 1945 and 1954, *State Library of Victoria*, Acc: H20475. Retrieved 5 June 2018 from: http://handle.slv.vic.gov.au/10381/294920

Unidentified. (2005). Inigo and Marion Jones in Their Garden at Crohamhurst, Ca 1935. *State Library of Qld.* Retrieved 3 June 2018 from URL: https://hdl.handle.net/10462/deriv/109403

Long-range weather forecaster, Inigo Jones, with Bernard Henry Corser at the opening of the Crohamhurst Observatory, ca. 1935. *John Oxley Library, State Library of Queensland.* Retrieved 3 June 2018 from URL: https://hdl.handle.net/10462/deriv/90481

Maps: ©OpenStreetMap contributors. www.openstreetmap.org/copyright

References:

1 *Said Hanrahan.* (1920, December 1). *Burra Record* (SA: 1878 - 1954), p. 3. Retrieved June 3, 2018, from http://nla.gov.au/nla.news-article39721083

2 Wikipedia contributors. (21 March 2018). Bushfires in Australia. In *Wikipedia.* Retrieved 23 March 2018 from URL: from https://en.wikipedia.org/w/index.php?title=Bushfires_in_Australia&oldid=831551394

3 Van den Honert, Rob; Oates, Lucinda; Haynes, Katharine; and Crompton, Ryan, A Century of Natural Disasters - What are the Costs? *Bushfire and Natural Hazards Crc*, 23 Jan 2015. Retrieved 3 June 2018 from URL: http://www.bnhcrc.com.au/news/2015/century-natural-disasters-what-are-costs

4 & 5 Insurance Australia Group, *Natural disaster costs to reach $39 billion per year by 2050*, 21 November 2017. Retrieved 3 June 2018 from URL: https://www.iag.com.au/natural-disaster-costs-reach-39-billion-year-2050

6 Sherratt, Tim, Inigo Jones: The Weather Prophet, *National Archives of Australia.* Retrieved 3 June 2018 from URL: http://www.naa.gov.au/collection/publications/papers-and-podcasts/prominent-people/inigo-jones.aspx

7 Burton, David, The Weather Prophet, 13 Feb 2017. *Your Trading Edge*, retrieved 3 June 2018 from: https://ytemagazine.com/the-weather-prophet/

8 Rainfall & Temperature Records, Australian Govt, *Bureau of Meteorology.* Retrieved 3 June 2018 from: http://www.bom.gov.au/climate/extreme/records.shtml

9 North Queensland Drought (25 Oct 1923). *The Register* (Adel, SA: 1901-1929), p5. Retrieved 8 April 2018, from http://nla.gov.au/nla.news-article65032621

10 Science Delegates Gather in Record Heat Wave (12 Jan 1939). *The Canberra Times* (1926-1995), p2. Retrieved 10 April 10 2018: http://nla.gov.au/nla.news-article2474300

11 THE HEAT WAVE (12 Jan 1939). T*he Canberra Times* (ACT: 1926-1995), p4. Retrieved 10 April 2018 from http://nla.gov.au/nla.news-article2474262

12 - 13 Sherratt, Tim. Op.cit.

14 Everybody Knows the Name (1 July 1954). *The Courier-Mail* (Bris, Qld: 1933-1954), p2. Retrieved 29 April 2018 from: http://nla.gov.au/nla.news-article50608324

15 THE LAND (20 Jan 1939). *The Land* (Sydney, NSW: 1911 - 1954), p11. Retrieved 10 April 2018, from: http://nla.gov.au/nla.news-article104157530

16 Flower, Horace, *Pastoral Review and Graziers' Record*, 16 Dec 1954, pp 1491 & 1493. Retrieved 3 June 2018 from: http://oa.anu.edu.au/obituary/jones-inigo-owen-539

17 & 18 Inigo Jones's Last Forecast (22 Nov 1954). *The Age* (Melb, Vic: 1854-1954), p. 1. Retrieved 13 April 2018 from http://nla.gov.au/nla.news-article205441877

19 Long-term temperature record Aust Climate Observations Reference Network – Surface Air Temperature, Australian Govt – *Bureau of Meteorology.* Retrieved 3 June 2018 from: http://www.bom.gov.au/climate/change/acorn-sat/#tabs=Data-and-networks

20 EVERYBODY KNOWS THE NAME (1954, July 1). Op.cit.

21 Wikipedia contributors. (13 Dec 2017). Crohamhurst Observatory. *In Wikipedia.* Retrieved 22 April 2018.

22 With Predictions Specially for our Readers... (22 Sept 1982). *The Australian Women's Weekly* (1933 - 1982), p 4. Retrieved 22 April 2018: http://nla.gov.au/nla.news-article52250850

23 'Jones, Inigo Owen (1872–1954)', Obituaries Australia, National Centre of Biography, *Australian National University.* Retrieved 30 April 2018 from URL: http://oa.anu.edu.au/obituary/jones-inigo-owen-539/text540

A boy with an axe, a tree with a past

Ewen Maddock & the Pandanus tree

Memorial: Monument of the Pandanus tree, Queen of Colonies Pde, Moffatt Beach, Caloundra, 4551.

Pandanus tree trunk on public display, first floor of the Commissariat Store Museum at 115 William Street, Brisbane

Interred: Ewen Maddock, 5 April 1873 – 1 August 1973 (aged 100 years).

Location: Section 2 South, Row 3, Site 29.

Cemetery: Mooloolah Cemetery, Steve Irwin Way (Glass House Mountains Road), Glenview, Sunshine Coast, QLD 4553.

This story is about a ship, a tree, a funeral and a boy with an axe. It is about dreams for a new beginning, orphaned children, a challenging rescue, castaway survivors, and an ambiguous carving of words on a tree. And it happened where today, tourists and residents alike swim and enjoy the beautiful surrounds of Caloundra.

Not many beach-goers probably stop to think about the name of the street they journey along – Queen of the Colonies Parade in the Sunshine Coast town of Caloundra. This street was named after the *Queen of the Colonies* ship; a 64-metre long clipper ship that sailed from London and Ireland with a cast of new Australians keen to start a life here – and a reasonable huddle of stowaways. It would harbour many stories of new beginnings, and for some, tragic tales of lives lost. Passengers aboard the *Queen of the Colonies* were no doubt abreast of the risks of seafaring adventures, but regardless, brimming with optimism, they set sail to begin the next chapter of their lives in Australia.

But there's more than adventure and tragedy involved in this tale, there's also a twist in the form of a Pandanus tree located on the headland at Moffat Beach. This tree was inscribed with the name of the ship by a shipwreck survivor or was it?

Away at sea

At the helm of the *Queen of the Colonies* was Captain Robert Cairncross. He set sail from London with 92 passengers onboard on Saturday, 13 December 1862. Detouring via Queenstown in Cork, Ireland, the *Queen of the Colonies* was boarded by an additional 158 passengers and this is also where a sizeable number of stowaways joined the voyage.[1] *The Courier* (Brisbane) wrote: "There appears to be a very general desire, amongst the Irish, to emigrate to this colony, as no fewer than twenty six persons secreted themselves on board the ship, at Queenstown, and they were not discovered for a considerable time after the vessel left the port."[2]

The *Queen of the Colonies* would become no stranger to sailing the route to Australia, doing so six times in the 1860s, and on one occasion, set a crossing record to Australia from England.[3] But in 1862, when our story is set, she was new to the voyage and set sail with Queensland in her sights.

Advertising card giving details of the ship, her sailing route, her owners, and other information, 1866. John Oxley Library, State Library of Qld.

Life and death onboard

On board were Thomas and Emma Barnfield, both 34, and their two children, Catherine, aged 7, and Tommy, just one. They were farewelled from their village in Somerset by family and friends—no doubt, some envious—to sail to a new life. The continuous rain and its effect on employment, and the low wages may have inspired Thomas and Emma to make the move, and as Emma had another baby on the way[4], life in Australia in 1863 no doubt seemed like a good idea.

But life is not put on hold while at sea for close to four months and despite the cramped conditions, the continuous rocking of the ship, and the watery world around them, there

Above: 'The Queen of the Colonies' sets sail. The original painting by artist Don Braben, can be seen in colour at the Queensland Maritime Museum.

were births, marriage celebrations and deaths. Distractions at sea were welcomed to fill the day, as documented by a passenger, H.H.C. Hurle:[5] "The first real bit of excitement was caused by our sighting two large ships, which we soon overtook, and passed… The 20th was a dull, uneventful, day, nothing to do but smoke and talk… By Friday… the sea was alive with flying-fish." There were many long days to fill.

Not long after departing Queenstown, a bout of measles became rife and worked its way through the passenger list with 35 cases reported, and six proved fatal for the infants on board.[6] *The Courier* noted: "There were also two deaths of adults in childbirth, one infant from convulsions, and one adult who died from injuries received by falling into the hold, thus making a total of ten deaths. By way of counterbalance to these losses there were seven births, five of which were females."[7]

Excited by the prospect of a new future, one couple tied the knot onboard, and the ceremony was officiated by Roman Catholic Chaplain, the Rev. Terence Joseph Quinn who came on board in Queenstown.

Emma's demise

Sadly, one of the noted deaths in childbirth was Emma along with her newborn, thus leaving Thomas a widower with two children. Her death cast a gloom over the ship's occupants.

The couple must have spoken about the prospect of death prior to taking the journey as Emma did not want to be buried at sea, and Thomas did his best to honour this request. But, it would be at the expense of his own life, and almost several crew members along with him.

Land ho and a burial party

When the ship finally arrived close to Queensland shores, there was now the opportunity to land and bury Emma; Thomas asked permission of the captain and he agreed. Passenger Mr Hurle recalls: "It was not permissible for her to be buried at sea, for the vessel was too close to land; furthermore her widowed husband wanted the body to be interred on land."[8]

At 5pm the next day, Tuesday 7 April 1863, just short of four months since their departure from England and while the *Queen of the Colonies* was anchored off the Cape Moreton lighthouse, Thomas along with 13 crew and volunteers, took the body of Emma in the lifeboat and paddled to shore to bury her.

Joining Thomas in the lifeboat were: "Captain [F.W.] Hill, and Messrs. Durrant, Arundel, Barnfield, Langford, Ford, Eldridge, (chief officer), Grant (fourth-mate), Roach and Murray (quarter-masters), and three able seamen."[9] Captain Hill would read the funeral service.

With the sad interment completed, the burial party set off for the ship about 7pm, and that's when disaster struck – an unexpected storm hit the returning funeral party, and the lifeboat and its passengers went missing. In his efforts to bury his wife, Emma, Thomas' life was at peril, along with the people who had gone ashore to help him.

The Courier reported:[10] "While going round under the stern to get to leeward of the ship, a violent squall drifted her away before the crew were able to catch a rope dropped to them by one of the passengers on board the ship. The boat was seen fruitlessly endeavoring to reach the ship again, but the wind carried her farther and farther away; and she was soon lost to sight in the surrounding gloom."

Mr Hurle wrote in his onboard diary: "The sailors rowed for all they were worth throughout the night, but, though they occasionally saw the ship's lights, they could not reach her."[11]

After a long night and morning of labour, the sailors had the *Queen of the Colonies* in their sight at 2pm on Wednesday 8 April 1863, but they still could not reach her. Their lifeboat drifted to shore at Mooloolah Beach and despite the strength of the surf, they got the boat ashore. Back on board the *Queen of the Colonies*, Captain Cairncross made the decision at 4pm to continue onto Brisbane and search crews were sent to find the crew and lifeboat.[12]

Left behind

That night the shipwrecked men camped and found some oysters on the rocks and a supply of freshwater, but little else in the form of food or infrastructure; they were hungry from days of exertion and exposure to the elements. They kept a fire burning, raised a flag in the hope it would be seen, and attempted to search for settlers or natives, without success. Scoping the area on foot, they covered about 10 miles but were held back by a river and swamp and forced to return to the original camp area.[13] No rescuers were in sight and their own rescue plans were proving futile.

The Courier reported three days after the disappearance and with the men still lost:

"As the wind was blowing off shore at the time, it is feared that the boat has been driven out to sea; but as she is

a life-boat and is managed by experienced seamen, we are inclined to believe she will return safely. As might be expected there were no provisions on board. Immediately the matter was reported to the authorities in Brisbane, the Acting-Colonial Secretary decided on sending the government steamer Brisbane to search for the boat." [14]

Water Police Inspector McDonald was in charge of the search. Meanwhile, on the following Tuesday 14 April, almost a week after they had been driven ashore, a change in conditions saw another chance at getting back to sea. The lifeboat was launched in the breaking surf and immediately swamped by heavy seas. It was an exhausting battle. This is when Thomas met his death. Some reports say he drowned while other sources, including a story by the Queensland Water Police, say he was taken by a shark and the remaining survivors hastily retreated to the shore. [15] Recalling the story 26 years later in 1889, *The Queenslander* newspaper reports the story of the missing crew and Thomas as such:

"The suspense and the privations which they were enduring becoming intolerable, they determined to launch their boat, which was high and dry upon the beach, and endeavour to find succour by that means. For this purpose they stripped themselves of their clothing except their shirts, and putting their cast-off garments into the boat, endeavoured to run her out through the breakers. In doing so, however, a heavy sea struck the boat and capsized her. This disaster resulted in the loss of all the clothing of which these unfortunate people had divested themselves, and to add to their grief Mr. Barnsfield, the husband of the woman they had buried on Moreton

Island, who had been conspicuous in his exertions in the attempt to launch the boat, was seized and devoured by two sharks before their eyes."[16]

Passenger Mr Hurle writes: "The small craft overturned and Barnfield, whose wife's burial had caused all the trouble in the first place, was never seen again. The others managed to struggle back to the shore."[17] Thomas and Emma's dream of a new beginning in Australia had ended in peril; their two remaining children on board the *Queen of the Colonies* were now orphaned in a new country.

A search party

As the men were all now weak and some suffering from exposure, hunger and dysentery, three of the more able men set off to find a means out of their situation. It was Thursday 16th April when Mr. Eldridge (first officer), Mr Grant (fourth) and Mr. Durant (a passenger) ventured off in a south-westerly direction battling swamps and unruly bush. But with no luck and failing strength, they were forced to return to their party. Arriving back at the camp on the 19th April, they found the site vacated, their party gone.[18]

What became of the lifeboat and the men aboard?

Water Police Inspector John McDonald was appointed to his role in late 1862, after serving as Acting Sergeant-in-Charge of the Brisbane Police Station.[19] Now, six months into the role, he was faced with the *Queen of the Colonies* rescue of fourteen missing passengers and crew.

One day, two days and eventually ten days passed and

Above: The original tree bearing the inscription 'Queen of the Colonies' at Caloundra. Source: State Library of Queensland.

still there had been no sign of the lifeboat nor the missing men. Not too many held hope for their survival. Regardless, Inspector McDonald and five of his men ventured onto the ocean in a rescue boat. Using oars, they were subjected to the weather and power of the sea and were almost shipwrecked themselves, resulting in their provisions being ruined by sea water and a near sinking in the Bribie passage.[20]

The Inspector and one of his team took to the land to search while the remaining men stayed with the boat. You can imagine the excitement and relief when the Inspector found the majority of the missing men at Caloundra Head – starved and exhausted, but alive.

Three remained missing as we know: Eldridge, Grant and Durant, who had gone on to try and find help for the group. And, this is where our Pandanus tree mystery comes into play. It is believed that one of these men inscribed on the Pandanus tree the words *Queen of the Colonies* and their initials in order to keep his bearings, to ensure they weren't going around in circles, and to find it on their return if their attempt to get to Brisbane was unsuccessful. But there's doubt as to the source of this inscription and we will look at that next.

Inspector McDonald took as many of the rescued men as he could safely fit into his boat and they were rowed off to safety. Fortunately, the steam-tug *Brisbane* arrived and took the remaining batch of survivors on board. Inspector McDonald returned to Caloundra Head with a fresh crew to pick up anyone remaining.[21]

The three lost men were now the target for the rescue party – Eldridge, Grant and Durant. They were eventually found, dehydrated, in rags, starving and of course sunburnt, sixteen days after the small party left the ship to bury Emma.

Inspector McDonald was rewarded and recognised for his efforts in the rescue with £100 from the owners of the *Queen of the Colonies*, and the Inspector was also presented with an expensive tea service with their gratitude.[22]

The mystery inscription

Many people would like to believe that the inscription on the Pandanus tree was made by a marooned *Queen of the Colonies* survivor. In 1889, *The Queenslander* newspaper reported that Inspector McDonald had made a mark on the tree carrying the carved message when he found the first group of shipwrecked men. The report says that Inspector McDonald:

> *"... felt compelled to remove them at once, leaving a pencil notice on one of the trees close by, saying that he would either return himself or send immediate succour... A Pandanus tree, still stands close to the place where they were found marked with the name of the ship deeply cut into the trunk by one of the shipwrecked crew. It was recognised and identified a few months ago by Mr. McDonald, who took his friends straight to the tree, though he had not seen it since 1860... This interesting and historical Pandanus tree, the record of a thrilling event which happened twenty-six years ago, will it is to be hoped be carefully preserved."[23]*

However, there's another theory of how the name came to be carved on the tree. Well-known Sunshine Coast identity, Ewen Maddock of Mooloolah, who contributed significantly in his adult life to the development of this region, is a 'contender' for having carried out the carving when he was a young boy in the 1880s.[24] Ewen (born 1873) claimed that after hearing the story from a teacher of the 1863 *Queen of the Colonies* journey, he used his axe—a birthday present—to carve the name into the Pandanus tree. While an axe may seem a strange present today, Ewen was five years old when he arrived in the Mooloolah area with his family, and working with his family on the land constructing fences, felling timber and driving bullock teams was a normal part of a farm boy's life, when he wasn't at school at the Mooloolah Plains Provisional school.

When *The Queenslander* reported that Inspector MacDonald took his friends straight to the tree, he may have recalled the tree he marked, and not necessarily the inscription, as many believed the bedraggled survivors would not have been carrying a tool suitable for carving. It is not known when Ewen claimed it was his carving, but it is likely he would have been between seven and 16 years of age at the time of carving the words, and 16 years old when the Inspector returned to the site.

What became of…

The Pandanus tree is no longer with us; the Landsborough Shire Council did their best to maintain the original tree until it died in the 1940s and its placed was marked by a formal concrete memorial in 1963, which you can view today.

Fortunately, thanks to the work of Queensland historians and the Royal Historical Society of Queensland, you can see the section of the tree trunk bearing the inscription *Queen of the Colonies* on public display at the first floor of the Commissariat Store Museum at 115 William Street, Brisbane.

Above: The original Pandanus trunk bearing the inscription is on display at the Commissariat Museum, William Street, Brisbane. Below: a group of men looking out to sea near the 'Queen of the Colonies' Pandanus tree at Caloundra, ca. 1905, 35 years before its demise. Source: John Oxley Library, State Library of Queensland.

Inspector McDonald remained with the Water Police for another four years before being appointed to the role of Superintendent of the Penal Colony at St Helena Island, where he stayed until his retirement in 1882.[25]

Reports on what became of Thomas and Emma's children varies. There is a record of death for one-year-old Thomas (Tommy) in the same year of the family's arrival in Queensland – 1863. He may not have survived the journey or died later that year.

Most accounts say that Emma Barnfield's baby died with her in childbirth, another account in the *Brisbane Courier*[26] in 1924 begs to differ, saying the three-week-old orphaned child, Katie, was reared by Barnfield relatives who lived in Fortitude Valley. However, there is no listing of Katie or a Katherine in the shipping records or birth records that we could find (only Catherine, the seven-year-old daughter). Perhaps the reference to the adopted child was meant to refer to seven-year-old Catherine, who was also nicknamed Kate.

Catherine was raised in Queensland and in 1877 at the age of 21, married Charles Frederick Smith. They had one daughter in 1884, named May Lillias, and Catherine died the year after[27] in 1885, aged 29 – a short but eventful life.

Ewen Maddock, the lad with his axe, is one of the Sunshine Coast's favourite sons and from a respected pioneering family of the area. Ewen Maddock Dam is named after him, and you can also visit the heritage-listed Ewen Maddock House Site at Maddock Park, Mooloolah Connection Road.

Ewen became very skilled with an axe; he left school early to work for his father as a timber getter. Also, with his father, Ewen worked on the construction of the North Coast Railway Line. He was one of nine children and his brother,

James, died of abdominal wounds received in action serving in France in World War I. Ewen married school teacher, Harriet, and lived to mark a centenary, dying in 1973 aged 100 years. He was buried in Mooloolah Cemetery with Harriett and other family members. The bunya pines that Ewen planted in 1900 still stand at the site of his home, and a replica of the cottage has been constructed.

How to find the monument:

A *Queen of the Colonies* plaque and the statue of the Pandanus tree can be seen on Queen of Colonies Parade, Moffatt Beach, Caloundra. You can see the original section of the tree trunk bearing the inscription 'Queen of the Colonies', on public display at the first floor of the Commissariat Store Museum at 115 William Street, Brisbane. The museum is open Tuesday to Friday from 10am to 4pm. Entry fees apply, guided tours are available. Visit: http://www.queenslandhistory.org/

How to find Ewen Maddock's grave in Mooloolah General Cemetery:

Ewen Maddock's grave is in Mooloolah General Cemetery, 8.5km east of Mooloolah towards Caloundra. The cemetery entrance is on the right-hand side of Glasshouse Mountains Road, just short of the Bruce Highway.

When you come off the Steve Irwin Way and into Mooloolah cemetery, stay on the bitumen and veer around to the right until you come to a car park. Immediately in from of the car park is small shelter housing memorial plaques.

Right behind that small, roofed building is a path that travels between graves... it leads off slightly to the right. Follow it for about 40 metres and you will find Ewen's grave on your right.

How to find Mooloolah General Cemetery:

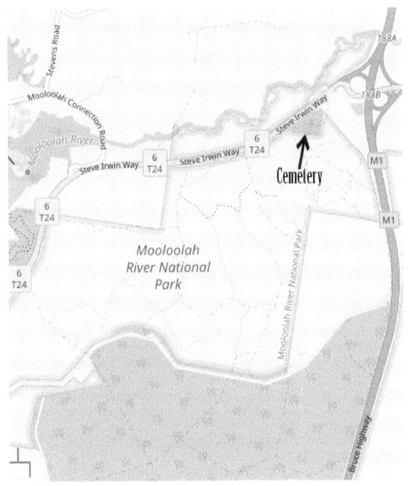

Map:©OpenStreetMap contributors. www.openstreetmap.org

The Queen of the Colonies monument at Moffat Beach, Caloundra.

References:

1 Hardie, Liz, Queen of the Colonies, 25 August 2015. *Hardie Family History*, retrieved online 18 May 2018 from URL: https://hardiefamily.atlassian.net/wiki/spaces/HFHW/pages/7536643/Queen+of+the+Colonies

2 THE QUEEN OF THE COLONIES. (1863, April 10). *The Courier* (Brisbane, Qld.: 1861 - 1864), p. 2. Retrieved May 12, 2018, from http://nla.gov.au/nla.news-article3162616

3 Hardie, Liz, Queen of the Colonies. Op.cit

4 Harrison, Jennifer. Mrs Barnfield and the 'Queen of the Colonies': The 1863 voyage [online]. *Queensland History Journal*, Vol. 22, No. 2, Aug 2013: 69-80. Retrieved 12 June 2018 from URL: https://search.informit.com.au/documentSummary;dn=469441633893967;res=IELHSS

5 Hurle, H.H.C. Queen of the Colonies, 1865. *Queensland Heritage*, Volume, No.6, 1967, p30.

6 & 7 THE QUEEN OF THE COLONIES. (10 April 1863). *The Courier*. Op.cit.

8 Hurle, H.H.C. Op.cit.

9 & 10 THE QUEEN OF THE COLONIES. (10 April 1863). *The Courier*. Op.cit.

11 Hurle, H.H.C. Op.cit.

12 Osborne, Sue, Queen of the Colonies, Voyages to Queensland: 1863. *Merriott Families Genealogy: History of Merriott and its People.* Retrieved 23 May 2018 from URL: http://merriottfamiliesgenealogy. net/about_me/queen_of_the_colonies/qotc-1863/

13 The Queen of the Colonies' Tree at Caloundra. (1924, December 6). *The Brisbane Courier* (Qld.: 1864 - 1933), p. 18. Retrieved 26 May 2018, from http://nla.gov.au/nla.news-article22887211

14 THE QUEEN OF THE COLONIES. (10 April 1863). *The Courier.* Op.cit.

15 Rice, John, *Queen of the Colonies,* 2009. Retrieved 23 May 2018 from URL: http://www.qldwaterpolice.com/history.html

16 A Reminiscence of the "Queen of the Colonies." (1889, June 22). *The Queenslander* (Brisbane, Qld.: 1866 - 1939), p. 1175. Retrieved May 24, 2018, from http://nla.gov.au/nla.news-article19815140

17 Hurle, H.H.C. Op.cit.

18 The Queen of the Colonies' Tree at Caloundra. Op.cit.

19 - 22 Rice, John. Op.cit.

23 A Reminiscence of the "Queen of the Colonies." Op.cit.

24 Osborne, Sue. Op.cit.

25 Rice, John. Op.cit.

26 The Queen of the Colonies' Tree at Caloundra. Op.Cit.

27 Family history research, *Queensland Government,* 11 May 2018. Retrieved 2 June 2018 from URL: https://www.qld.gov.au/law/births-deaths-marriages-and-divorces/family-history-research

Images:

'The Queen of the Colonies', oil on canvas, by Don Braben. Courtesy of Queensland Maritime Museum, and reproduced with the kind permission of the artist.

Unidentified Queen of the Colonies Tree, Caloundra. *John Oxley Library, State Library of Queensland.* Retrieved 26 May 2018 from URL: https://trove.nla.gov.au/work/153928183

Unidentified (1905). Group of men looking out to sea near the Queen of the Colonies Pandanus tree at Caloundra, ca. 1905. *John Oxley Library, State Library of Queensland.* Retrieved 26 May 2018 from URL: https://trove.nla.gov.au/work/153915561

Unidentified (1866). Queen of the Colonies (ship). *John Oxley Library, State Library of Queensland.* Retrieved 26 May 2018 from URL: https://trove.nla.gov.au/version/47902925

Maps: ©OpenStreetMap contributors. www.openstreetmap.org/copyright

The stretcher bearer
Henry Buchanan

Interred: Sergeant Henry Buchanan, 14 July 1889 –
11 March 1953 (aged 63 years).

Location: Five rows from the timber gazebo, in line
with two pine trees *(see picture)*.

Cemetery: Tewantin Cemetery, Cooroy Noosa Road,
Noosa Shire, QLD 4565.

Sgt. Henry Buchanan MM - 9th Infantry Battalion. Photo donated by Sgt. Buchanan's great nephew, Damon Bickle, author of 'The Fields of Pozieres'.

It's a long way from the mines of Gympie to carrying a stretcher on the battlefields of Gallipoli, but that's where 25-year-old Henry Buchanan found himself after enlisting once the war was declared. What Henry would do, and what he would face, would terrify any person – and he lived to tell.

Life as he knows it

Henry's life in Gympie from his birth to enlistment no doubt focussed on work, family and his crowded house. He was the youngest of 10 children – his father died in 1890 when Henry was one, and his mother, Annie, died in 1903 when Henry was 14. Nevertheless, he followed in his father's footsteps to work in the mines – a major employer for the town.[1] The pulse of Gympie was beating fast; it was only declared a town in 1903, the graziers had settled it. James Nash discovered gold there, creating a wave of gold rush fever and saving the state from bankruptcy; the Gympie Hospital opened two years after Henry's birth, in 1891, and in the same year Gympie was linked to Brisbane by the North Coast Rail. Gympie was going places and so was Henry.

It was August 1914 when Britain and Germany went to war, the Great War it was called then, and Australia pledged support. There was excitement and enthusiasm amongst many young men who thought it would be a great adventure; 416,809 of our men enlisted, including Henry. More than 60,000 would be killed and 156,000 would experience a wounding, gassing or imprisonment by the enemy.[2] Henry would distinguish himself in ways he would never have dreamed of before donning his Australian army uniform.

Three weeks after war was declared, Henry signed up and a month later he sailed on the *HMAT Omrah* to join the fight. His service would be as a stretcher bearer, running onto battlefields to remove the injured, often at the mercy of shells bursting close by. His brother, Malcolm, was listed as his next of kin in the absence of his parents.

Henry was one of the soldiers on the HMAT Omrah as it departs the Pinkenba wharf, Qld, 1914. Source: John Oxley Library, State Library of Queensland.

Wounded in action

It was at Gallipoli, where Henry had been serving for almost eight months, when in May 1915 he was first wounded in the right elbow.[3] He was out of action for the month and returned to his unit on 1 June. For the next four months he ducked and weaved with his stretcher, bringing the injured back to care, until taking a bullet that caused a compound fracture and his own evacuation to a hospital in Cairo.[4] It was now October 1915; he had been at war for a year and shot twice. As a stretcher bearer, Henry was listed as a non-combatant but in his own words, Henry said he had been "mixed up in some scraps"[5] and he had the bullet and bayonet wounds to prove it.

When he was fit to return to duty, Henry was assigned to the 49th Battalion. It was made up of Gallipoli veterans from the 9th Battalion like Henry, and fresh reinforcements from home, mainly from Queensland.[6] With a promotion to Corporal, Henry and his fellow soldiers set sail for France, arriving on 12 June 1916.

Henry and the Germans on the Western Front

With nearly two years of service under his belt, Henry faced the first battle at Pozieres with gusto and experience. The 49th moved into the trenches of the Western Front for the first time on 21 June. What a year it would be; Henry's battalion suffered heavily and throughout the remainder of the year, they fought on the front line, laboured behind the lines and suffered through a horrendous winter.[7]

As a stretcher bearer, Henry was privy first hand to the

agony of the newly wounded, and generous in his praise of his fellow soldiers' stoical suffering: "In France I attended a bad case. A South Australian, who returned by the same boat, was hit by a whizz-bang shell. I was standing close by and immediately went to his aid. There were 46 separate wounds, 42 of which were received from the hips down. I had no morphia, but he did not even lose consciousness."[8]

Australian stretcher bearers coming in under a white flag, passing the old cemetery of Pozieres, having come from the line near Mouquet Farm, August 1916. Maker: Ernest Brooks, source: Australian War Memorial.

A stretcher bearer's perspective

Seeing many of his comrades in agony and no doubt carrying many of them on his stretcher in their final moments, Henry took the time to pen a letter to grieving parents. It was picked up by The *Brisbane Courier* and ran in November 1915. Here's an extract which illustrates his role and that of fellow stretcher bearers:[9]

"YOUR SON DIES A HERO."
STRETCHER BEARERS' HEROISM
A BRAVE MAN'S TRIBUTE TO A BRAVE COMRADE.

Mrs. H. J Scoones, Church street, Red Hill, has received the following letter from Private H. Buchanan, written from Gaba Tepe, Gallipoli :

"Dear Mrs. Scoones, I am sure you must think we are rather a poor lot for not writing to you before this giving you a few details of your son George's death. It is only a few weeks since we had permission to do anything of the kind so, I hope you will forgive us for our neglect. The first thing I am able to say is that your son died a hero. I was with him at the time he was wounded, also when he passed away.

"At the time he was wounded he and myself were on our way across an open patch to attend a wounded man. When about half way across we came to a very dangerous spot. A Turkish machine gun started to play over our heads, and I called out, 'Down Scoones,' both of us lying on our stomachs. We remained there about half a minute until the gun ceased. Up we got again, and had just started to run when they opened on us again. They had been waiting for us. However, we kept on going, as it was useless to get down again. When almost to safety I heard a groan and saw George stumble and fall. I lifted him up and carried him to safety. I was between two fires.

"He said , 'What are you going to do with me? I said, 'You will have to be taken back the way we came.' He would not hear me risking my life across the open patch but, I had my duty to do, so after waiting a few minutes until the firing eased off a bit I picked him up and started back. When the Turks saw me carrying a wounded man they never attempted to interfere. However I managed to get George back to the doctor (Captain Butler), who did all that was in his power, but George lapsed into unconsciousness shortly after and passed away quietly.

"His last words to me were to thank me for all that I had done for him. 'Thank you, old chap; you did your best, but I don't like my chance.' He is buried in our little cemetery, where we have erected a cross over his grave. I have taken a photo of it, and will send you a copy first opportunity. All my comrades wish me to express their deepest sympathy with you. That you may be able to bear up in your hours of grief is the wish of us all."

A bluff and a cool head

Maybe Henry learnt how to bluff to get attention as the youngest of 10 children, or maybe he picked it up in his school years, but that skill would save his life. When stretcher-bearing at Mouquet Farm, he stumbled across the enemy and not only tricked his way out of the situation but took the enemy prisoner. *The Sydney Morning Herald* reported the medal-winning heroism:

"In the thick of an attack he accidentally entered a German dugout while searching for wounded, and, much to his surprise, found eighteen Germans*, three of whom were officers, well-armed. Here the narrator paused,

"Well, I bluffed them," he said. "The Germans were as much surprised as I was."

He took a bottle out of his pocket and held it up as though it were a bomb.

"If you don't come out I'll bring you out," he said.

The Germans came out of their shelter one by one, and were subsequently sent to the back of the lines. For this exploit Sergeant Buchanan was awarded a further decoration in the shape of a bar to his Military Medal."[10]

In the letter penned recommending a Military Medal for Henry, the incident was further described as such:

"This N.C.O. was in charge of the stretcher bearers and personally conducted them through heavy shell and rifle fire to the front line before communication was established to evacuate the wounded. During one of his trips in searching a dug out for wounded he came across 2 Officers and 11 other Ranks Germans* whom he took prisoners and marched to the rear. My front line and support line were kept free from wounded, and it was entirely due to the N.C.O. in charge of the stretcher bearers that it was so. When one considers that during

the two days fighting over 300 casualties evacuated from Y sector the work done by the stretcher bearers will be fully appreciated."[11]

(*Source: Commonwealth Gazette No. 62 Date: 19 April 1917.* *Note the discrepancy in the number of Germans in two reports).

Home for a brief while

Henry took his third bullet, a gunshot wound to the foot in September 1916 and less than two weeks later was promoted to Sergeant. In October, Henry was awarded the Military Medal for his actions at Mouquet Farm.[12]

It seemed impossible to keep Henry down; he was wounded the next month with a gunshot to the hand and while he rejoined his unit momentarily, Henry needed medical attention and returned to Australia in August 1917.[13] It had been three years since he was home, and what he had seen and done in that time was incomparable to his former mining life.

With some local encouragement and the desire to give fellow soldiers a voice, Henry agreed to enter politics and stand for the seat of Barcoo. But in his own words: "I'm glad to be back, but, if the doctor says 'yes', I'm going back again."[14] And the doctor did say yes, so Henry put his political career on hold and returned to the front for another year before his medical discharge in December 1918.[15] He was now 29 years old. One of Henry's big brothers, Thomas, did not survive the war, dying in 1916 aged 37.

Two years later, Henry married and with his wife, Gwen, moved to Sandgate. They had three sons, returning to

Gympie and then moving on to Cairns. When World War II broke out, Henry enlisted again as a Warrant Officer Second Class; he was 50 years old. Surviving his second major war, Henry and Gwen moved to Tewantin and Henry took on the role of President of the RSL. He passed away aged 63, in Tewantin on 11 May 1953; Gwen died two years later.

Some might say Henry Buchanan had more lives than a cat, and you have to wonder if any of his German captives ever knew—or would admit—that they were rounded up with a makeshift bomb in the shape of a bottle!

The Daily Mail in 1917 best summed up this modest Australian hero who went to war as a stretcher bearer and came home a hero:[16]

"Two hundred Queensland returned soldiers arrived in Sydney this morning, and left by special train at 11.15 for the North. There were many who had received decorations, but the hero of the train was Sergeant H. Buchanan."

Above: Could one of these men be Henry? Australian soldiers in trenches at Gallipoli, 1915, probably stretcher bearers of the 9th Battalion AIF. [Joseph Cecil Thompson - presumed photographer]

How to find Henry's grave in Tewantin Cemetery:

To avoid some of the 'tourist' traffic, the easiest way into Tewantin Cemetery is via the Cooroy turnoff. When you enter Cooroy-Noosa Road, you will find two entrances to the cemetery. They are both fine to enter, but the entry with the 'Tewantin Cemetery' sign above it is closer to Henry's grave. Drive/walk in and park near the gazebo. Look for two large pine trees and in line with that is Henry and Gwendoline's grave. It is about five rows in from the Gazebo, features white tiles and is a 'double' size (see photo page 42).

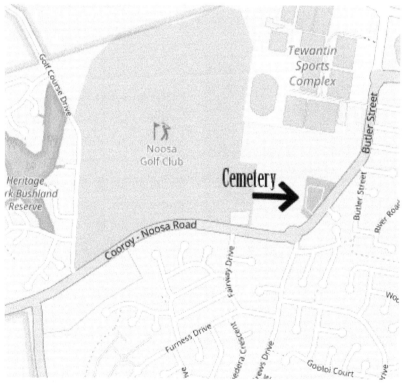

Map:©OpenStreetMap contributors. www.openstreetmap.org

References:

1 Buchanan, Henry, *Adopt a Digger Project*, retrieved 2 June 2018 from URL: http://www.adoptadigger.org/search-for-a-ww1-digger/search-for-a-ww1-digger/item/3-diggers-database/2387-buchanan-henry

2 First World War 1914–18, *Australian War Memorial,* retrieved 2 June 2018 from URL: https://www.awm.gov.au/articles/atwar/first-world-war

3 & 4. Buchanan, Henry, *Adopt a Digger Project.* Op.cit.

5 SOLDIERS' RETURN. (1917, September 20). *The Sydney Morning Herald* (NSW: 1842 - 1954), p. 8. Retrieved June 2, 2018, from http://nla.gov.au/nla.news-article15755234

6 & 7 - 49th Australian Infantry Battalion, *Australian War Memorial,* retrieved 2 June 2018 from URL: https://www.awm.gov.au/collection/U51489

8 SOLDIERS' RETURN. (20 September 1917). Op.cit.

9 WITH OUR BOYS. (20 Nov 1915). *The Brisbane Courier* (Qld: 1864-1933), p. 6. Retrieved 2 June 2018 from http://nla.gov.au/nla.news-article20082960

10 SOLDIERS' RETURN. (20 September 1917). *The Sydney Morning Herald* (NSW: 1842-1954), p8. Retrieved 2 June 2018, from http://nla.gov.au/nla.news-article15755234

11, 12 & 13. Buchanan, Henry, *Adopt a Digger Project.* Op.cit.

14 SOLDIERS' RETURN. (1917, September 20). Op.cit.

15 Buchanan, Henry, *Adopt a Digger Project.* Op.cit.

16 A GYMPIE HERO. (1917, Sept 21). *The Daily Mail* (Bris, Qld: 1903-1926), p6. Retrieved 1 June 2018 from http://nla.gov.au/nla.news-article215259881

Images:

Sgt. Henry Buchanan MM, 9th Infantry Battalion. Photo reproduced with kind permission from Sgt. Buchanan's great nephew, Damon Bickle, author of *The Fields of Pozieres:* https://thefieldsofpozieres.com/

Unidentified (1914). Soldiers on the deck of the HMAT Omrah as it departs the Pinkenba wharf, Qld 1914. *John Oxley Library, State Library of Qld*, retrieved 2/6/18 from: https://trove.nla.gov.au/version/225058856

Ellen Thompson (1915). Australian soldiers in trenches at Gallipoli, 1915, probably stretcher bearers of the 9th Battalion AIF. [Joseph Cecil Thompson - presumed photographer] Retrieved 7 October 2018 from URL: https://trove.nla.gov.au/version/255375350

Brooks, Ernest, Australian stretcher bearers, Pozieres, August 1916. Australian War Memorial. Retrieved 7 Oct 2018 from URL: https://www.awm.gov.au/collection/E04946/

Maps: ©OpenStreetMap contributors. www.openstreetmap.org/copyright

Why isn't it Nashville?
The James Nash story

Interred: James Nash, 5 September 1834 – 5 October 1913 (aged 79 years).

Location: CES –7–336.

Cemetery: Gympie Cemetery, Corella Road, Gympie, QLD 4570.

James Nash, 1868. Source: John Oxley Library, State Library of Queensland

If it's true that Australia rode to prominence on the sheep's back, then it is equally true that Queensland got there in the miner's ore cart… and this is a part of that story.

It centres on a man by the name of James Nash who arrived in Brisbane from NSW when the state was just five years old and had already gone through some financial ups and downs. Stories abound that the NSW government had left just seven and a half pence (about $2.20[1]) in the Queensland Treasury when the state was given its independence in December 1859[2]. And, furthermore, on the 27th of the same month, The *Empire* newspaper in Sydney reported that the *Brisbane Courier* had carried a story that said those few coins were stolen from the state coffers! *"The Treasury offices were burglariously entered by some venturous thief. But, luckily, he only succeeded in walking off booty to the amount of seven pence in coppers."*[3]

Now the story has done the rounds ever since that the seven pence was the entire wealth of the state of Queensland at that time and it was the gold discovery at Gympie, made by James Nash, which solved the embarrassing situation that left the state entirely bereft of funds…. flat broke.

Some sources say Queensland was so poor that Governor Bowen had to put his hand into his own pocket to pay the state's first public servants[4], but the next line in the *Brisbane Courier* story seems to indicate there was more money there to be had: *"The cashbox from which these coins were taken, seemed to have puzzled the burglar, or else the loss would have been greater."*[5] The other complicating factor in the theory that Nash got Queensland out of strife in 1859 is that he didn't make his 'Hallelujah' strike until 1867... but there's no doubt his discovery did significantly contribute to resolving Queensland's financial calamity when land-based business hit hard times.

Cattle and trains

To understand how the state got into so much financial trouble by the mid-1860s, it is necessary to see just how much reliance government placed on pastoralism – that is, raising livestock. Colonial administrations were increasingly involved in pastoral promotion believing that eventually small block farming or closer settlement* would be the predominant development. While manufacturing was generally left to its own devices, parliamentarians and administrators were active in promoting railways and pastoral development... and borrowing heavily to do it.

But by the middle of the 1860s a series of droughts which had struck over previous years finally led to pastoralists becoming over-extended and the state economy was in crisis. And when the droughts just kept on coming and land prices plummeted, weighed down by the burden of its borrowings, the state was technically bankrupt.

The Bank of Queensland closed its doors and on Good Friday 1866 the state observed a day of: "Humiliation and Prayer... in consequence of the long-continued drought in this colony; and which has been the means of bringing much distress upon the inhabitants."[6]

By now the unemployed were marching in the streets of Brisbane and regional towns... there were plenty of them and they were angry. In September there was a riot in Brisbane when a navvy by the name of William Eaves, took it upon himself to address the enraged mob. He said: "We did not come here to be paupers, nor to accept of charity, but to work and work we cannot get, and bread we cannot do without - and bread we will have - if we don't get bread we will have blood. And bread or blood we will have tonight – let us do it now."[7]

But the government had no money for bread... or for infrastructure projects... and the situation was exacerbated by the continuing arrival of immigrants... up to one thousand a month who had been, up until this financial crisis, largely employed on public works.

The government's pride and joy, the first railway line which was being built between Ipswich and Toowoomba, was also a victim when work was halted. One newspaper described the atmosphere in the nation's newest capital city:

"NEVER since Queensland became an independent colony has there been such a general feeling of alarm and distrust among her colonists."[8]

Things were now beyond tough and in desperation in January 1867, the state government offered a 3000 pound reward for the discovery of a new payable goldfield. There were confusing conditions attached to the offer. Some reports say it would have to be within 90 miles of Brisbane... others, 50 miles... and some sources say the reward was only one thousand pounds for a goldfield that would support 500 men after six months of operation.

Gold! Just in time...

Whether he considered the offer motivation enough... or just a bonus if he struck gold... James Nash was on the road.

Nash had left school in his native England at the age of nine to take up a job keeping the rooks off fields of beans in the aptly named village of Beanacre, Wiltshire, where he was born in 1834. He left England when he was 23 and arrived in Sydney on 25 May 1858. After working around the North Shore and trying his hand at several goldfields, he set his eyes on Queensland, arriving in 1864.

By 1866 he was actively involved in the search for a payable goldfield and eventually ended up at a place we now know as Caledonian Hill in Gympie. In those days it was prickly scrub above a creek in a gully where Nash tried his luck. On the first day, he got a few flecks of colour, (as gold traces are called) and the next day collected over an ounce in his dish. On day two of the exploration, he broke his pick and so set out for Maryborough to sell the small amount of gold he had found and buy a new pick and some rations. He went back to the same place and over the next six days gathered over 75 ounces of gold which he was picking up in small pieces rather than tiny flecks.

James Nash must have started to believe that he may have found something worthwhile – a gully at least that was delivering good alluvial gold... maybe there would be more. He took the 75 ounces and again headed for Maryborough but this time to take a steamer to Brisbane to get the tools and provisions he would need to ensure he had found the real thing.

In Brisbane he bought a horse and dray, and a sluicing cradle for separating gold from the sand and gravel found in creek beds, and set out for his gully of hope once more. He and a young man named Malcolm, who he met on his way back to Brisbane, worked the area for almost two weeks before Nash headed for Maryborough yet again… this time carrying with him a large bag of gold. He must have been getting anxious after he sold the 75 ounces of gold in Brisbane that word would leak he was onto an Eldorado… a place of fabulous riches.

He went straight to the Maryborough Police Magistrate, Richard Sheridan on Monday 14 October. The Magistrate sent a police officer and party to what was to become known as 'Nashville' to peg out the claim. They marked his original claim and one and a half bonus claims as a reward for finding a commercially viable deposit. It became known as Nash's Gully.

The gold rush begins

On Wednesday 16 October 1867 James wrote to the Minister of Lands claiming the 3000 pound reward for the discovery of a payable goldfield. He wrote: "I do myself the honour to inform you that I have found a gold field in the Wide Bay District…" [9] On the same day his find was announced… and the rush was on.

It is said that within a week Maryborough was all but deserted and there were three hundred men on the track to 'Nashville'. By November the rush was on in earnest and no doubt many of those who were unemployed because of the drastic state of the economy, also made their way by whatever means they could to the diggings… and clearly some, if not all of them, were ill-equipped.

A report by a Police inspector by the name of Lewis was quoted in the *Brisbane Courier* on 14 November 1867. He wrote:

"On reaching the diggings I found a population numbering about five hundred, the majority of whom

were doing little or nothing in the way of digging for the precious metal. Claims, however, were marked out in all directions, and the ground leading from the gullies where the richest finds have been got was taken up for a considerable distance. I have very little hesitation in stating that two-thirds of the people congregated there had never been on a diggings before, and seemed to be quite at a loss what to do. Very few of them had tents to live in or tools to work with; and I am afraid that the majority of those had not sufficient money to keep them in food for one week."[10]

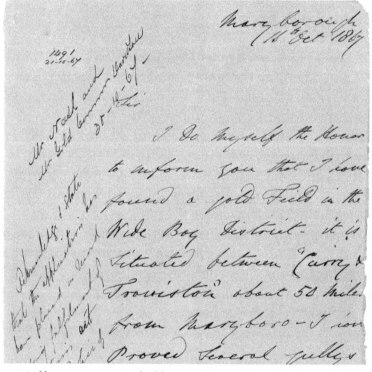

James Nash's announcement of gold, 1867. Source: Queensland State Archives.

And now that thousands were heading north, the old mountain track to Gympie that went through Canondale, Obi Obi, and Traveston, and was described as 'something frightful', was simply not good enough... as the inspector pointed out:

"I am quite satisfied that no loaded dray could possibly have reached the diggings safely, were it not for the assistance of parties of men proceeding to the gold-field... several drays were overturned, and some of the drivers badly bruised in their attempts to save the horses and goods entrusted to their charge from destruction. I was very much surprised that no lives were lost in these hazardous undertakings, more especially as I found that it was with much difficulty I managed to lead on foot a saddle-horse along some of the places where drays had passed."[11]

Most making their way to the field were taking the steamer to Maryborough and then trekking from there. A decent road must be a priority.

Initial doubting suspicions over the long-term viability of the 'Nashville' field were quietened when large amounts of gold began to emerge and the second wave of would-be miners started to arrive. Within a few months, there were 15,000 on the field.[12] The fears of longevity were also allayed with the discovery of the Curtis Nugget... the biggest lump of gold ever unearthed in Queensland. It was found not far from where James Nash had first tried his hand... it weighed 975 ounces... or nearly 27.5 kilograms and was valued at 3675 pounds or in purchasing power, about $418,000 today.[13]

Nashville in all its glory

In 1868 'Nashville' was little better than a mining shanty town of tents and crudely built bark and paling humpies, many of which were little bigger than two metres square. There were many small shops and of course liquor outlets... and the produce from them was the source of much of the trouble in the place. Drunken brawls were commonplace and attacks often left the recipients in dire straits: "Between Thursday night and Friday morning at a shanty some distance from the One-mile main street, occupied by persons of the name of Boyle, a most disgraceful outrage took place, by which a miner by the name of Michael Dalton was severely wounded and knocked about... a more savage attack has seldom been perpetrated, and the guilty parties may have to expiate their brutality on the gallows as doctors called in have not expressed any certainty as to the result not proving fatal."[14]

And there were also bushrangers to fear on the tracks in and out... this from the *Queensland Times* on 11 April 1868:

"La Barte and Co's coach left Nashville as usual yesterday morning, at about 6 o'clock, with thirteen passengers; at about 7 o'clock, and when nearly three miles on this side of the diggings, as the coach was rising a hill, the driver was challenged by three persons under arms, who bade him 'stop'. Unfortunately, as it happened, there was neither a gun nor a revolver among the company in the coach, and the order to 'Get down and shell out quickly' was submissively and expeditiously obeyed." [15]

Still, Nashville continued to grow and as the settlement went from a shanty town to one with wealth and some degree of style about it, James Nash made a lot of money... somewhere in the vicinity of 7000 pounds or nearly 800,000 dollars today.[16] He and his brother lost all of it in an ill-conceived drapery business. And he didn't get his 3000 pounds 'reward' for discovering the gold field either. The government argued that he didn't meet all the conditions... and it turned into a protracted dispute. After a 12-month battle, James ended up with just 1000 pounds... a pittance considering the amount of gold extracted in the life of the Gympie field and the rich underground operations that sprang from the original James Nash discovery.

The value of the gold extracted up until 1927, when the field practically ceased to be an active gold producer, was 14,296,320 pounds[17] – in today's terms that would have the purchasing power of around $1,056,200,000[18]... an extraordinary amount of money in anyone's terms. It's

Nashville around 1867 - 1868 in Mary Street, near the intersection with Channon St. Source: The Brisbane Courier, Queensland State Archives.

understandable why the Gympie goldfield was hailed as the discovery that saved Queensland. The huge injection of capital into the community provided hope and was the financial salvation of the state.

Nash, the man…

As for the man who made it all possible, it seems until he struck pay dirt James Nash was pretty much a dedicated prospector, not afraid to take to the road with his swag, his pick, panning dish and ever loyal dog. He walked thousands of kilometres in his travels around the country. He was always on the move and until his Gympie strike did not have a permanent place he called home… and even then, he didn't stay put for long.

Less than a year after his amazing discovery, in July 1868, Nash married Catherine (Kate) Murphy whose father owned a pub. A couple of months later he sold his claim and took his wife to England to meet his family.[19] There are claims that it was at this time—while he was out of the country—that the name of the place where James had discovered gold was changed from Nashville to Gympie… apparently the Aboriginal name for a local stinging tree.

Three of James and Kate's children died young… three survived to adulthood. One of the lads, Herbert, was deaf and mute as a result of a childhood accident and the other, Allan, who had two children of his own, joined the AIF and was killed at Gallipoli in 1915.[20]

It wasn't long before James Nash found himself in dire financial difficulties and his friends intervened, appealing to the government, which in 1888 appointed him keeper of the Gympie powder magazine at a salary of one hundred pounds a year. James Nash died in Gympie on 6 October 1913 at the age of 79 and is buried in the Gympie Cemetery. Kate Nash lived until 1931 and after James' death was awarded a 50 pound per year pension by the state government. James Nash was a quiet, unobtrusive man and apparently liked to recount tales of his life as a prospector... and there would be plenty willing to wager an ounce of gold or two that high on the list would be the story of how he found the big one that saved the state.

How to find Gympie Cemetery & James' grave at CES–7–336:

Enter through the main gate on Corella Road. To your right you will see the cemetery buildings and James Nash lies between those buildings and the cemetery fence. The grave is painted white and stands out. It is four rows from the fence line and 46 metres from the entrance roadway. There is also a memorial to James Nash in Memorial Park, at the intersection of Reef Street and Rivers Road in Gympie.

Map:©OpenStreetMap contributors. www.openstreetmap.org

Closer settlement is a policy of settling areas so that in a normal season a landholding is just large enough to support a family comfortably. The policy assumes that small holdings, whether held by individuals or cooperatives, realise the land's full potential, usually via agriculture, and that people can easily come together to support markets, schools, churches and other civilised amenities.

References:

1 Hutchinson, Diane and Ploeckl, Florian, *Five Ways to Compute the Relative Value of Australian Amounts, 1828 to the Present, Measuring Worth*, 2018. Retrieved 4 June 2018 from URL: www.measuringworth.com/australiacompare

2 Moore, Tony, "New South Wales left Queensland broke from day one", *Brisbane Times*, 6 August 2017, first published 28 July 2017. Retrieved 11 March 2018 from URL: https://www.brisbanetimes.com.au/national/queensland/new-south-wales-left-queensland-broke-from-day-one-20170728-gxl38l.html

3 QUEENSLAND. (1859, Dec 27). *Empire* (Sydney, NSW: 1850 - 1875), p.5. Retrieved 11 March 2018, from URL: http://nla.gov.au/nla.news-article64095070

4 Moore, Tony. Op.cit.

5 QUEENSLAND. (1859, December 27). *Empire*. Op.cit.

6 SOCIAL. (1866, April 17). *The Brisbane Courier* (Qld: 1864 - 1933), p2. Retrieved 11 March 2018 from URL: http://nla.gov.au/nla.news-article1265855

7 Wilson, Paul, D., The Brisbane Rot of September 1866. *Queensland Heritage*. Retrieved 4 June 2018 from URL: https://bit.ly/2Hj2UJU

8 THE FINANCIAL CRISIS IN QUEENSLAND. (1866, July 24). *The Sydney Morning Herald* (NSW: 1842 - 1954), p. 5. Retrieved March 11, 2018, from http://nla.gov.au/nla.news-article13134315

9 James Nash's announcement of gold at Gympie, 16 October 1867. Retrieved 4 June 2018 from *Queensland State Archives*, Digital Image ID 2766.

10 GYMPIE CREEK GOLD FIELDS. (1867, November 14). *The Brisbane Courier* (Qld.: 1864 - 1933), p. 2. Retrieved March 12, 2018, from http://nla.gov.au/nla.news-article1288519

11 GYMPIE CREEK GOLD FIELDS. (1867, November 14). Op.cit.

12 Death of Mr. James Nash. (1913, October 18). *Northern Star* (Lismore, NSW: 1876 - 1954), p. 9. Retrieved 13 March 2018 from URL: http://nla.gov.au/nla.news-article72340510

13 Hutchinson, Diane and Ploeckl, Florian. Op.cit.

14 LIFE AT GYMPIE. (1868, October 9). *The Brisbane Courier* (Qld: 1864 - 1933), p. 3. Retrieved March 12, 2018, from http://nla.gov.au/nla.news-article1332148

15 THE HIGHWAY ROBBERY NEAR GYMPIE. (1868, April 11). *Queensland Times,* Ipswich Herald and General Advertiser (Qld: 1861 - 1908), p. 3. Retrieved March 12, 2018, from http://nla.gov.au/nla.news-article123355499

16 Hutchinson, Diane and Ploeckl, Florian. Op.cit.

17 Laurie, Arthur, The Drama And Romance of the Gympie Goldfield, *Queensland Historical Society* 30 August 1962. Retrieved 4 June 2018 from URL: https://bit.ly/2JdGQC8

18 Hutchinson, Diane and Ploeckl, Florian. Op.cit.

19 -20 Ferguson, John & Brown, Elaine, The Gympie Goldfields 1867-2008. *Gympie Regional Council.*

Images:

Unidentified (1868). James Nash, 1868. *John Oxley Library, State Library of Queensland*. Retrieved 4 June 2018 from URL: http://hdl.handle.net/10462/deriv/205727

[Photographer unidentified], Gympie, c1868, *The Brisbane Courier.* Queensland State Archives, Retrieved 4 June 2018 from URL: https://www.flickr.com/photos/queenslandstatearchives/26779159304/in/photolist-MB6Hhj-Wn5sfm-GNoc6b-WtbWiW-XcNtLQ-WC5ASV-HBd2Vh-WLQc1h-WQ6qpH-LSvNFs-VoxKCr-L5VE1G-LQGnBQ-LXk4MA-dwLHfe/

James Nash's announcement of gold at Gympie, 16 October 1867. Retrieved 4 June 2018 from *Queensland State Archives*, Digital Image ID 2766.

Maps: ©OpenStreetMap contributors. www.openstreetmap.org/copyright

Mystery at the mine
George Argo

Interred: George Argo, 30 March 1841 - 21 February 1895 (aged 54 years).

Location: PS-10-110.

Cemetery: Gympie Cemetery, Corella Road, Gympie, QLD 4570.

One can't help but think that Scottish mine manager, George Argo, was a likeable man. He stood up for the workers, put his own shoulder to the grindstone, and even gave the feminists something to smile about by taking Lady Musgrave—the Governor's wife—on a tour of the mine.

So, who would want to cause him harm? And how did a man so conscious of safety fall to his death in the mine he managed? After all, he knew every inch of the No.1 North Phoenix mine in Gympie. He was a respected manager and experienced miner, and succeeded in closing almost every mine in the region on the day of his funeral as the workers came to pay their respect. But to this day his 'accidental' death, over a century ago remains a mystery.

A day like any other day

It was a Thursday, a typical day at work at 9am on 21 February 1895 – a day like any other day. George's morning began like most of his mornings; he arrived at work, did his regular inspections, and gave instructions about what had to be done above ground before going below to do his inspections there.

By his side was Mr Mawby, an engineer, who went below ground first on the brace, as George preferred to go down alone.[1] Engineer Mawby got out at about 70 feet below ground level. Then George was lowered down to about 240 feet. *The Coolgardie Miner* reported:[2]

"About five minutes afterwards, the engine driver heard someone call out "On top!" The engine driver called out "Hullo," but got no reply: he saw the rope shake, and called out, again, but still got no answer. The engine

driver told him he thought some man had fallen down the winze. The men working at the 820ft. level who had heard something fall down the winze [a shaft or passage], had gone; to ascertain what it was, and found the manager lying... dead."

The manager was George Argo and he was brought to the surface and examined by two doctors who found extensive injuries: a broken neck, both legs and one arm broken, and his skull was smashed in several places. They concluded his death must have been instantaneous."[3]

The Barrier Miner (a broadsheet newspaper published in Broken Hill in far western New South Wales from 1888) received a telegram advising of George's death and reported: *"He fell down a winze and was killed instantaneously."*[4] The *Coolgardie Miner*[5] provided more information:

"At first the report was received with incredulity, but unfortunately its correctness admitted of very little doubt. No one appears to have been with Mr. Argo at the time he met his death, and hence the accounts heard during the day were conflicting, though all agree on one point – namely, that the immediate cause of Mr. Argo's death was a fall down the deep winze from the 666ft. level, on the Smithfield reel."

A man of stature

George and his wife, Elizbeth, hailed from Scotland, and George was no stranger to hard labour or mines. In the early 1860s he worked on the Ipswich to Toowoomba railway, before working in Gympie's Deep Lead mine – a relatively

*Above: Gov. Musgrave's visit to no. 1 Phoenix Mine, 6 June 1888. Reproduced with kind permission from the Gympie Regional Council Library Service. Circled is **George Argo** and seated front row L to R is: Major Ferguson (Mayor), Mrs Ferguson, **Sir Anthony Musgrave, Lady Musgrave**.*

Below: View of One Mile, Gympie, 1895. Source: State Library of Queensland.

76

unprofitable venture. His next mining adventure was in New Zealand and proved to be most profitable – the mine is said to have reached the peak of its production while he was manager. George and Elizabeth then ventured to England and it was on his return that he began the fateful role in the management team at the No. 1 North Phoenix mine in Gympie.[6]

George was an influential man; in fact, the most influential men in the town were the mine managers as not only were these men responsible for hiring and firing, but they were often shareholders. George made some influential contacts including the man he replaced, who left to enter Parliament – William Smyth. George and William formed the Gympie Mine Managers' Association. Their role as explained in the book *'The Gympie Goldfield: 1867-2008'*[7] was to: "Discuss such matters as safety issues and government regulations. If necessary, they lobbied the authorities for changes and improvements... provided opportunities for influential managers to liaise with the local community, the government and other goldfields. It can also be seen as a response to the formation of unions among the ordinary miners."

George *(circled left)* also personally gave the Queensland Governor Sir Anthony Musgrave's wife, Lady Musgrave, a tour of the underground workings of the mine. It was not the 'done thing' for a woman to enter the mines and George was a part of Lady Musgrave's ground-breaking precedent![8]

Fine tributes

As a measure of his regard, the city of Gympie turned out in force for his funeral parade; 1500 mourners, including 400 horsemen paid their respect. *The Queensland Times* wrote: "The length of the procession can be imagined when it is stated that it took half an hour to pass a given spot."[9] *The Brisbane Courier* continued: "*With a few solitary exceptions, where bailing was being carried on, all the mines were shut down and employees attended the funeral.*"[10]

After George's death, accolades abounded. He was remembered as: "A ruler among men; all who came within his influence felt it, and acknowledged it, and all, willingly or unwillingly, submitted to his guidance and control."[11] And a man with "a strong energetic will, a clear and capacious mind,"[12] a man who put "his own shoulder to the wheel, for whatsoever his hand found to do, he did it with all his might."[13]

The mystery remains

No one could say how it happened and no-one ever stepped forward with an alternative theory. The irony is not lost on many, however, that a man concerned with safety should meet his demise as a result of a mining accident.

George had no children of his own, but was twice married and raised Emma, the daughter of his first wife, Julia, who died in 1878.[14] George lies in the Gympie cemetery with his second wife, Elizabeth [of Bligh Street] described as: "One of the leading supervisors in the Benevolent Society, and an ardent worker."[15] She died 27 years after George.

George's grave has been known to glow at night... fans of a ghostly tale will tell you it will continue to do so until the mystery of his death is solved.

How to find George's grave at PS-10-110, Gympie Cemetery:

You can't miss the tall Argo tombstone. Enter through the main entrance from Corella Road. Travel about 130 metres, passing the cemetery buildings on your right. Turn right at the next intersection, travel 140 metres until you come to an unmade track off to the right. Continue towards the boundary fence and you will find George Argo's grave off to your right, about 20 metres before reaching the boundary.

References:

1 - 3 The Death of Mr. Argo. (28 Mar 1895). *Coolgardie Miner* (WA: 1894 - 1911), p3. Retrieved 1 June 2018 from: http://nla.gov.au/nla.news-article216259421
4 DEATH OF MR. GEORGE ARGO (1895, February 22). *Barrier Miner* (Broken Hill, NSW: 1888 - 1954), p. 2. Retrieved June 1, 2018, from http://nla.gov.au/nla.news-article44176981
5 The Death of Mr. Argo. (1895, March 28). Op.cit.
6 - 8 Ferguson, John & Brown, Elaine, *The Gympie Goldfield*: 1867-2008. Gympie Regional Council (Qld.) 2009. Retrieved 6 June 2018 from: https://www.gympie.qld.gov.au/documents/40005057/41317496/Gympie%20Goldfields%20Book%20Complete.pdf
9 Death of Mr. G. Argo. (1895, February 26). *Queensland Times*, Ipswich Herald and General Advertiser (Qld.: 1861 - 1908), p. 4. Retrieved June 6, 2018, from http://nla.gov.au/nla.news-article130379186
10 SOUTH BRISBANE FIRE BRIGADE. (1895, February 26). *The Brisbane Courier* (Qld.: 1864 - 1933), p. 4. Retrieved June 8, 2018, from http://nla.gov.au/nla.news-article3597516
11- 13 Original Correspondence. (23 Feb 1895). *Gympie Times and Mary River Mining Gazette* (Qld: 1868-1919), p3. Retrieved 1 June 2018 from URL: http://nla.gov.au/nla.news-article171742622
14 Ferguson, John & Brown, Elaine. Op.cit.
15 GYMPIE. (31 October 1922). *The Brisbane Courier* (Qld.: 1864-1933), p10. Retrieved 1 June 2018, from: http://nla.gov.au/nla.news-article20580613

Images:

Unidentified (1895). Goldmine at One Mile, Gympie, 1895. *John Oxley Library, State Library of Queensland*. Retrieved 6 June 2018 from URL: https://trove.nla.gov.au/version/47938002
Unidentified (1888). Governor Musgrave's visit to no. 1 Phoenix Mine, 6 June 1888. Gympie Regional Council. Reproduced with kind permission of the *Gympie Regional Council Library Service*. Retrieved 6 June 2018 from URL: https://trove.nla.gov.au/version/94192911

In Loving Memory of

CECELIA ELIZABETH
BAUER.
DIED JUNE 6th 1905.
AGED 22 YEARS.

In Loving Memory
of
ROSE ADELAIDE
[NURSE ADELA]
BELOVED DAUGHTER OF
CHARLES AND MARY A. WILES
WHO, ON 12th JUNE, 1908,
PASSED ON
"TO BE WITH CHRIST, WHICH IS FAR BETTER."
ALSO OF
MARY A. WILES,
MOTHER OF THE ABOVE
AND DEARLY BELOVED WIFE OF
CHARLES WILES,
WHO FELL ASLEEP, ON 28th JAN. 1910
IN HER 89th YEAR.
"BLESSED ARE THE DEAD WHICH DIE IN THE LORD."
"I AM THE RESURRECTION AND THE LIFE."
JOHN 11.25
AND OF
REV. CHARLES WILES
BORN 7th MAY 1837. FELL ASLEEP 8th FEB 1918
FOREVER WITH THE LORD.

THE O'CONNELL FAMILY

Black death pays a visit
The O'Connell family
Nurses Cecelia Bauer & Rose Wiles

Interred:

The O'Connell family children:
- John, 1888 – 25 May 1905 (aged 17 years);
- James, 1891 – 31 May 1905 (aged 15 years);
- Ellen Bridget, 1898 – 31 May 1905 (aged 7 years);
- Richard, 1893 – 2 June 1905 (aged 12 years*);
- Johanna Mary, 1902 – 3 June 1905 (aged 3 years).

Cecelia Bauer, 1883 – 6 June 1905, (aged 22 years).

Rose Adelaide Wiles, 1877 – 12 June 1905 (aged 28 years).

Letitia Edwards, 1856 –31 May 1905 (aged 49 years).

(*On the O'Connell family monumental headstone in Maryborough Cemetery, Richard's age at death is listed as 10 years, but the Queensland Birth Registry[1] lists Richard's birth year as 1893, which would make him 12 at the time of his death).

Location:

Monumental F:
- John O'Connell – Plot 1069.
- James and Ellen O'Connell – Plot 1068.

Monumental T:
- Richard O'Connell – Plot 24.
- Johanna O'Connell – Plot 11.
- Nurse Cecelia Bauer – Plot 36.

Monumental C:
- Nurse Rose Adelaide Wiles – Plot 609.

Monumental L:
- Mrs Letitia Edwards – Plot 12.

Cemetery: Maryborough Cemetery, cnr Walker Street & Bruce Highway, Maryborough West, QLD 4650.

It wasn't the dark ages, nor was it a time before adequate sewerage – it was 1905 and Maryborough—country of the Gubbi Gubbi and Wakka peoples—was a modern city, with impressive architecture and a major port of entry, thanks to the Mary River. But regardless, the Black Death paid a visit.

The pneumonic plague comes to call

The first case of plague (bubonic) in Australia was reported in Sydney in January 1900. Getting on the front foot, the Maryborough Municipality purchased the defunct Dundathu Sawmill Village and converted it to the Dundathu Plague Hospital and Quarantine Station.[2] Fortunately it was not used.

However, in a wide, diverse country, Maryborough was the only place in all of Australia to record an occurrence of the pneumonic plague and it had a lethal impact, particularly on one family and the two nurses who would care for them. But it won't surprise you why, when you combine the factors. Maryborough was the largest port in Queensland[3] – here all manner of goods, and people, came and went.

The pneumonic plague differed from the bubonic plague... it was a life-threatening infectious disease which humans could spread easily, as simply as by sneezing. The symptoms were easily noticeable: fever, weakness, headaches, and coughing up mucus from the lungs. You can imagine how quickly a disease of this nature could fell an entire population.

It was 3 June 1904 when a man was taken to the Maryborough Hospital with these symptoms and died soon after (note he was not taken to the Dundathu Plague

Hospital which had become a 'white elephant'). While his death certificate did not list plague as the cause, the Government Medical Officer, Dr J. A. C. Penny, suspected otherwise and ordered the fumigation of the victim's house and of the isolation ward in the hospital where he died.[4] His actions may have saved hundreds, even thousands from the deadly disease, but more victims were to come.

Local baker, John Rillie, who worked in Adelaide Street, fell ill with the plague symptoms next and Dr Penny had him, the bakery and its staff isolated immediately. There was no avoiding word getting out now as police officers were stationed at the front and back of the building to ensure that the staff did not leave[5] – a terrible waiting game for all involved.

Adelaide Street, Maryborough in 1904, the site of John Rillie's quarantined bakery. Source: State Library of Queensland.

The local paper, *The Maryborough Chronicle,* appealed for calm, and fortunately John Rillie had not baked his last loaf; he recovered and for almost a year the city recorded no further cases and residents began to breathe easy.

The plague returns

But in winter 1905 the plague made an 'official' visit to Maryborough. A family by the name of O'Connell was the first to be felled. Their situation was summarised by Dr B. Burnett Ham in his report to the Department of Public Health Queensland as: "Consisting of seven children, residing with their father at Newtown, near the city, in a state of great poverty and neglect – father out of employment, and of intemperate habits; mother dead."[6] The O'Connell family's mother, Ellen, passed away aged 39, just eighteen months before the plague hit her family; not living to see five of her seven children succumb to the illness.

The head of the family, Richard, was known to hit the bottle and was often absent from the family home. The eldest son, John, had a job but regardless, John and his siblings Kate, James, Ritchie, May, Ellen and Mary were no strangers to poverty or scavenging. So when their father, Richard, brought home some sacking from the wharf for his children to sleep on, they were welcome additions for bracing against the winter conditions. There was speculation that the sacking, if infected, may have contributed to the family's deaths, along with the death of a neighbour and two young nurses.

A family felled

John was the first to be struck down and of course calling a doctor was out of the question unless it was an absolute emergency... money was short. It wasn't until John had suffered at home for five days that Dr John Crawford Robertson called on him. It had been a year since plague symptoms were last seen in Maryborough, but dengue fever was rife, and John was diagnosed with the same.

John didn't improve, and his sister Kate ran to the neighbours for help. The generous neighbour, Mrs Letitia Edwards, 49, nursed John but by the morning of Friday 26 May, he had passed away.[7] His cause of death was certified as pneumonia.[8]

MARYBOROUGH.

Friday.

CASE OF PLAGUE.

In connection with the recent cases of suspicious illness in Maryborough Dr. Tyrie, of the Health Department, arrived this afternoon from Brisbane, in company with Dr. Penny, Government Medical Officer, and made a close inquiry, and as a result has pronounced the case of a girl, aged 19 years, residing in Kent-street, in the centre of the city, to be one of true plague. The cause of the recent deaths in the O'Connell family has not yet been determined. Another member of the O'Connell family died in the General Hospital to-night after a short illness. The plague patient will be removed to the Plague Hospital to-morrow.

The outbreak of plague has occasioned great surprise, and every precaution is being taken by the authorities to check it.

The O'Connell case is determined as plague as reported on 3 June 1905 by The Brisbane Courier.

However, Dr Ham notes in his report: "This boy was employed as an assistant in a fruiterer's shop situated in the main thoroughfare of the town. An open sewer—a natural watercourse—receiving the main drainage of the city, runs beneath and alongside a block of shops, including the fruiterer's shop referred to, and affords an excellent harbourage for rats."[9]

The O'Connell family had suffered the loss of their mother and eldest born son, and now four of the remaining six children were ill with the same symptoms as John: "headache, pyrexia [fever, high temperature], severe vomiting, pains in the cardiac and epigastric regions."[10] However, this time, Dr Crawford returned on the 28 May and immediately hospitilised the family.

On this same day two of the children—Richard (Richie), aged 10, and Mary, aged three—were taken to the home of a friend of the family, Miss Schafer, but not for long. Soon Richie and Mary fell ill and were admitted to the General Hospital by their father.[11] The kind actions of the neighbour, Mrs Letitia Edwards who had nursed John and laid out his body, would come back to haunt her; she was now also showing the same symptoms and was admitted to the hospital.

Five days had passed since John's death, when on 31 May Ellen, aged seven, and James, 15, died in their hospital beds. Mrs Edwards would die the same day. Dr Ham received a telegram that very day from Dr. Penny (Government Medical Officer at Maryborough) saying:[12]

"Boy and girl died at hospital. Woman who attended also died, all of broncho-pneumonia, after three days' illness. Two sisters and one boy still ill in hospital Suspicious. Want post mortem examination on woman."

Dr Ham telegraphed back: *"Take all precautions. Isolate cases and contacts as far as possible. Send 'specimens' of organs from post mortem case here for examination. Will send my Health Officer and serum if symptoms still suspicious. Wire me progress today."* The same day (1 June) the reply came back by telegram: *"Precautious taken... think plague."*

A ray of hope for the O'Connell family

There was a ray of hope, when the eldest O'Connell daughter, Kate, 18*, and her younger sister May, aged nine, both recovered enough to be discharged. They would be the only two survivors of the O'Connell siblings. (*Kate or Catherine is listed as 18 in all media coverage, but according to her birth certificate was born in 1885, making her 20 at the time of the outbreak).

But young Richie and Mary, who were the last two admitted, died on 2 June and 3 June respectively, both with symptoms of plague-pneumonia. The pathology report from the postmortem for young Richie O'Connell was sent to Brisbane; Richie's body showed all the signs of pneumonic plague, as did Mary's remains, but confirmation from Brisbane had not yet arrived.

At the hospital, the brave staff of doctors and nurses, and the other patients were exposed to the children and their neighbour. But yet, no one had officially diagnosed any of the six children or Mrs Edwards with pneumonic plague.

A vulnerable lifestyle

The lifestyle of the children made them particularly susceptible to the virus. Dr Ham observed:

"The squalid surroundings of the O'Connell family—the majority of the family were practically dependent upon the charity of neighbours—their ill-nourished bodies, and insanitary dwelling abode (the Municipal Inspector reported that the interior of the house was in a filthy state), were doubtless predisposing causes in lowering individual vitality and the natural resistance to infection."[13]

He noted that the kindly neighbour, Mrs Edwards, who attended the eldest son, John, would have contracted the plague by "drop-infection – the atmosphere immediately surrounding the patient containing minute suspended particles of expectoration." And that fortunately the friend of the family, Miss Schafer, did not come to the house until after John's death and thus escaped infection. [14] The children had been exposed to John for a week before his death, notwithstanding, Kate and May survived. Miss Schafer gave another perspective:[15]

"The children were in the habit of picking up fruit thrown about the streets, and especially near the sewer at the rear of the shop where John [eldest brother] worked. All had been eating 'specked' fruit brought home by John. May, Jim, and Ritchie were eating raw sweet potatoes on Sunday, 28th May, when I went there. I took Jim, Ritchie, and Mary to my home on the Sunday, as Kate, Nellie, and May had been sent to the hospital, and there was no one to mind them… Mary was vomiting all the night, and Jim and Ritchie had terrible pains in the chest and head. I lay alongside the two boys on the bed, with Mary in my arms. None of the children had cough or spat out anything whilst they were at my home."

Fortunately, the very brave Miss Schafer did not fall victim to the plague. Kate O'Connell, 18, the eldest daughter said: "Neither I nor May (the only two members of the family who survived) ate raw sweet potatoes just before we took ill, but all the others did, even the baby."[16] Dr Ham noted that "uncooked sweet potatoes are a foodstuff especially attractive to rats, and often used by the departmental rat-destroying gang as baits for cages and traps."[17]

On 3 June the authorities headed to the home of the late Mrs Edwards, fumigated the building and burnt clothes and bedding; the O'Connell house was next, burnt down by the fire brigade. The citizens of Maryborough turned out in force to watch, there was now no hiding that the plague had returned to Maryborough and already taken its toll.

They gave themselves

Two young nurses put their lives at risk—perhaps unknowingly at first as the official diagnosis had not been recorded—to nurse the patients with the plague – the O'Connell children and Mrs Edwards.

Nurse Cecelia Elizabeth Bauer, 22, was a staff nurse on night duty, and Cecelia was placed in charge of the O'Connell family from the day of their admission. She was no stranger to big families as one of ten children herself – she had four sisters and five brothers. Her father was Felix Bauer, a German born immigrant, and her mother, Mary Ann, was from Ireland.[18] Cecelia was engaged to be married in six weeks' time to William Hastings.

Nurse Rose Adelaide Wiles, 28, also known affectionately as Nurse Adela, was the third daughter of Mary Ann and Reverend Charles Wiles[19] and the first to put her hand up to nurse the victims.[20] But within a couple of days both Cecelia and Rose begin to show the symptoms; both had long-term significant exposure to the children.

Believe it or not, the ward was still not officially isolated despite the best efforts of staff, thus exposing all hospital staff to the threat. As the health of the two nurses declined, more staff and resources were called for, but Cecelia and Rose would not allow the new nursing staff near them.[21] Nevertheless, Nurse Elizabeth (Eliza) Sprague, 28, did attend to them at the risk of her own health.

From left to right: Nurse Elizabeth Sprague, Nurse Cecelia Bauer, and Nurse Rose Adelaide Wiles, photo taken 1905. Reproduced with kind permission from the Wide Bay Hospitals Museum Society Inc.

On Tuesday 6 June, Cecelia died; three days after coming down with the symptoms. And, on the same day, confirmation arrived from the Brisbane pathology lab that the sickness was the pneumonic plague... two weeks after the first victim died. That is, two weeks where countless people may have been exposed if it had not been for the compassion of Nurses Rose and Cecelia, the action of the doctors, and the Council with their diligence.

The Staff at Maryborough General Hospital, April 1905 – a poignant photo taken just months before the deaths of Nurses Cecelia Bauer (back centre) and Rose Adelaide Wiles (seated, far right). Nurse Elizabeth Sprague is in the far left, back row. Reproduced with kind permission from the Wide Bay Hospitals Museum Society Inc.

Rose was next to develop "clinical symptoms of lobular pneumonia with cough and watery sputum."[22] She clung to life for six more days, dying on Monday 12 June, nearly one week after Cecelia. The newspaper reported:

"Matters in connection with the outbreak of pneumonic plague have taken a most regrettable turn... and we have to announce the death at the General Hospital at an early hour this (Monday) morning of Nurse Wiles, after an illness of but a few days' duration. The news of the death of this popular nurse, who was a daughter of Rev. C. Wiles, of Maryborough, will come as a shock to the community. We regret to state that one of the nurses who had been attending Nurse Wiles is also seriously ill, but so far her case has not been definitely diagnosed as plague. The strict quarantine on the hospital still continues.... Dr. Ham, accompanied by Dr. Love left Brisbane tonight for Maryborough to further investigate the mysterious illness."[23]

The Hospital Committee would later receive a letter from Rose's father, Reverend Wiles, thanking them for their sympathy and "The courage and fortitude of their demeanour during the severe strain of the memorable days through which they had so lately passed had evoked the highest admiration." He noted: "The special kindness shown by Dr. Lee Garde and the Matron he and his family would never forget." The Reverend enclosed £5 5s., "with a desire that there should be recorded in the minutes and annual report the following: — *In memory of my dearly beloved daughter, Rose Adelaide (Nurse Wiles), who fell at her post of duty on June 12th, of pneumonic plague, contracted while ministering to pneumonic plague patients in the Hospital. 'She gave Herself.'*[24]

Above: Nurses tending to isolated plague cases, 1905. Below: Specially devised overalls and respirators worn by Dr. Burnett Ham and his staff. Source: State Library of Queensland.

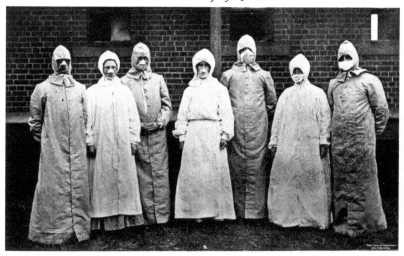

Nurse Eliza Sprague battled all the tell-tale symptoms, but fortunately recovered and was discharged.

Tackling the problem

Now all relevant hospital staff members were given an injection of Yershin's Serum – a serum developed by Swiss-born French bacteriologist Alexandre Yersin against plague in human beings and cattle.[25] Any nurses showing symptoms were removed from the environs and made a full recovery. No other cases were recorded.

In May – June 1905, Dr Ham presented a full report on the outbreak for the Queensland Department of Health and its impact on "a city of 12,000 inhabitants".[26] He noted:

"The measures taken for the suppression of the outbreak were preventive inoculation of doctors and nurses in attendance, and the wearing of specially designed costumes and respirator; isolation of the infected; segregation of the probably infected (quarantine of the hospital premises); destruction by burning of O'Connell's house with its contents; disinfection of clothes; disinfection of houses, including the General Hospital; cleansing operations, and the destruction and examination of rats... It is to be regretted that the precautionary measures taken by the Department of Public Health, and which were carried out with success after the death of the seventh patient, could not have been enforced at an earlier date."[27]

Dr Ham concluded that the quarantine period was strictly observed; all wards of the hospital were disinfected;

the ward that housed Nurse Cecelia and the O'Connell children was eventually released from quarantine; and no more cases were recorded. He noted rat catching gangs had only found two rats that were plague-infected. But Maryborough received a thorough clean.

The lack of postmortems for several victims did not assist with identifying the disease and was dealt with swiftly. As early as 1901—four years before the O'Connell deaths—all medical officers received a circular saying: "Any sudden death occurring during a plague epidemic, or threatened epidemic, should be regarded as suspicious, and a postmortem examination made."[28] After all, a registration of death cannot be truly final without a cause of death listed. Had Mrs Edwards been given a postmortem the disease might have come to light earlier, possibly allowing for better precautions, especially for nurses Cecelia and Rose. Instead, she was buried "without a death or other certificate."[29]

The Maryborough Cemetery rules and regulations said no funeral was to take place without the appropriate death certificate but Harry Nicholas Hansen, sexton at the cemetery, stated: "If I do not receive the certificate the undertaker generally tells me ' it is alright.' I cannot very well stop a whole congregation outside the gate if there is no certificate. I have let in many funerals without a certificate a score of times."[30]

Remembering their sacrifice

If it were not for the bravery of Cecelia, Rose, Eliza, the matron and doctors, in continuing their care for the O'Connell children and Mrs Edwards in as best an isolated state as manageable, many, many more would have suffered.

Today Cecelia and Rose, who continued their care despite the consequences, are remembered with a memorial fountain on Lennox Street. The wording reads:

To honour the memory of
NURSES BAUER AND WILES
who gave their lives nursing the victims
of an outbreak of pneumonic plague
"The Black Death" in June 1905

You can pay your respects at their graves in Maryborough General Cemetery. If you would like more information, seek out the documentary *Black Death*, produced in 1986 by Douglas Fraser and Tony Matthews and remastered on DVD.

What became of…

Of the two surviving **O'Connell siblings**, 20-year-old Kate (Catherine) and nine-year-old May, finding Kate has proven challenging, but it appears she may have married Francis McIvor in 1910 at the age of 25; her age at death is unknown. May married Martin Woods in 1918 at the age of 22, and died in 1963, aged 67 years.

Some time after her death, **Nurse Cecelia Bauer's fiancé, William,** went to America where he found work on the construction of the Golden Gate Bridge. He accidentally fell from the bridge to his death[31]– he was one of 11 workers who died during its construction.[32]

Nurse Eliza Sprague continued nursing, remaining for almost a decade at St Mary's Hospital (the forerunner to St Stephen's). She also worked at a military hospital in Brisbane's Kangaroo Point during the First World War.[33]

How to find the O'Connell family grave, Monumental F, Plot 1068 and 1069:

Enter the cemetery off Walker Street through the gate furthest from the Bruce Highway. Go towards the Mortuary Chapel *(pictured below),* when you come to it take the second path to the left (about 100 metres from the gate). Walk down about 40 metres and the O'Connell family are off to your right.

Nurse Cecelia Bauer's grave, Monumental T, Plot 36:

Enter the cemetery off Walker Street through the gate furthest from the Bruce Highway. Go towards the Mortuary Chapel *(pictured below),* when you come to it take the second path to the left (about 100 metres from the gate). Travel almost as far as you can go... about 130 metres and you will find Cecelia's grave off to your left.

Nurse Rose Adelaide Wiles' grave, Monumental C, Plot 609:

Enter the cemetery off Walker Street through the gate furthest from the Bruce Highway. Go towards the Mortuary Chapel *(pictured right),* when you come to it, turn down the road that runs left. Travel approximately 70 metres and you will find Rose's grave off to your right.

How to find the Maryborough Cemetery at the corner of Walker Street and the Bruce Highway (marked with X):

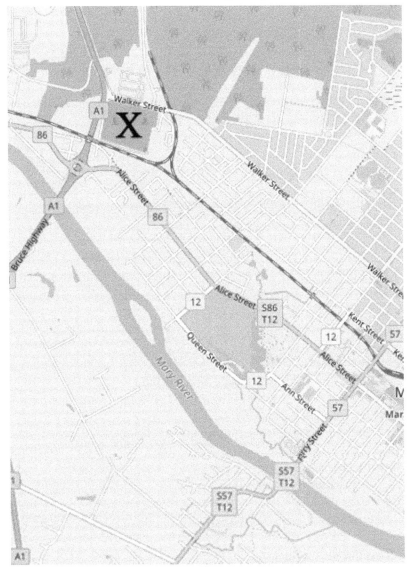

Map:©OpenStreetMap contributors. www.openstreetmap.org

References:

1 O'Connell births, Queensland Birth, Deaths and Marriages, *Queensland Government.* Retrieved 14 June 2018 from URL: https://www.bdm.qld.gov.au

2 DUNDATHU PLAGUE HOSPITAL. (28 July 1900). *Maryborough Chronicle, Wide Bay and Burnett Advertiser* (Qld.: 1860-1947), p2. Retrieved 7 Oct 2018 from http://nla.gov.au/nla.news-article147782008

3 Black Death in Maryborough 1905, *Fraser Coast Libraries Local History Blog,* 11 Aug 2011. Retrieved 14 June 2018 from URL: http://fclibrarieslocalstudies.blogspot.com/2011/08/black-death-in-maryborough-1905.html

4 – 5. Ibid.

6 Ham, Burnett, B., M.D., Report on the outbreak of plague in 1905. *Queensland Department of Public Health,* Brisbane, May – June 1905. Retrieved 14 June 2018 from URL: https://archive.org/stream/b21351582/b21351582_djvu.txt

7 – 17. Ibid.

18 Meyers, Lynn, Private Walter Frederick Bauer of Tiaro, 11 January 2016, SL Blogs, *State Library of Queensland.* Retrieved 14 June 2016 from URL: http://blogs.slq.qld.gov.au/ww1/2016/01/11/private-walter-frederick-bauer-of-tiaro/

19 Family Notices (17 June 1905). *The Telegraph* (Brisbane, Qld: 1872-1947), p 6 (2nd ed). Retrieved 15 June 2018, from http://nla.gov.au/nla.news-article174212405

20 Black Death in Maryborough 1905. Op.cit.

21 Ibid.

22 Ham, Burnett, B., M.D. Op.cit.

23 Pneumonic Plague at Maryborough. (1905, June 13). *Gympie Times and Mary River Mining Gazette* (Qld.: 1868 - 1919), p. 3. Retrieved June 14, 2018, from http://nla.gov.au/nla.news-article188058277

24 THE HOSPITAL COMMITTEE. (13 July 1905). *Maryborough Chronicle, Wide Bay and Burnett Advertiser* (Qld.: 1860 - 1947), p3. Retrieved 14 June 2018, from http://nla.gov.au/nla.news-article148677283

25 The Editors of Encyclopaedia Britannica, Alexandre Yersin, *Encyclopædia Britannica*, 22 February, 2018. Retrieved 14 June 2018 from URL: https://www.britannica.com/biography/Alexandre-Yersin

26 Ham, Burnett, B., M.D. Op.cit.

27 – 30. Ibid.

31 *The Gordon Family Tree.* Retrieved 14 June 2018 from URL: http://members.iinet.net.au/~janlar/gordonfamily/gordonfam/pafn108.htm

32 Klein, Christopher, 6 Things You May Not Know About the Golden Gate Bridge, *History,* 25 May, 2012. Retrieved 14 June 2018 from URL: https://www.history.com/news/6-things-you-may-not-know-about-the-golden-gate-bridge

33 Jensen, Marilyn, *Wide Bay Hospitals Museum Soc. Inc.*, conversation 15 June 2018 and *Fraser Coast Chronicle article*: 'Readers help identify nurse from early 1900s', 7 May 2017. Retrieved 15 June 2018 from URL:https://www.frasercoastchronicle.com.au/news/chronicle-readers-help-identify-nurse-early-1900s/3175040/

Images:

Nurses Sprague, Bauer and Wiles with staff at Maryborough General Hospital, April 1905. Reproduced and identified with kind permission from the *Wide Bay Hospitals Museum Society Inc.*, https://www.facebook.com/widebayhospitalmuseum (*Individual photos of the three nurses featured on page 91 are extracted from this photo).

Unidentified (1905). Nurses tending to isolated Plague cases, Maryborough, 1905. *John Oxley Library, State Library of Queensland.* Retrieved 13 June 2018 from URL: Nurses tending to isolated Plague cases, Maryborough, 1905

Unidentified (1905). Specially devised overalls and respirators for Maryborough outbreak (Primary Pneumonic Plague), May-June, 1905. *John Oxley Library, State Library of Queensland.* Retrieved 13 June 2018 from URL: https://trove.nla.gov.au/version/167838506

MARYBOROUGH. (3 June 1905). *The Brisbane Courier* (Qld.: 1864 - 1933), p. 5. Retrieved June 13, 2018, from http://nla.gov.au/nla.news-article19310238

Unidentified (1904). Adelaide Street Maryborough, looking west, ca. 1904. *John Oxley Library, State Library of Queensland.* Retrieved 15 June 2018 from URL: https://trove.nla.gov.au/version/47944779

Maps: ©OpenStreetMap contributors. www.openstreetmap.org/copyright

In Loving Memory of
MOLLIE
THOMPSON
DIED 11TH AUG. 1942

ALSO MOTHER
DIED 8TH NOV. 1952

The mystery of Mollie
The Mollie Thompson story

Interred: Mary Josephine (Mollie) Thompson, 1918 –
11 August 1942 (aged 24 years).

Location: Section - Monumental FR, Plot/Niche - 108.

Cemetery: Maryborough Cemetery, Walker Street,
Maryborough, QLD 4650.

It may well have been the most curious morning of Violet Madsen's life. Did she do a double-take when she saw Mollie Thompson treading lightly down Bazaar Street Maryborough at six o'clock on a cold August morning? Did she wonder what the 24-year-old girl was doing… no shoes and dressed only in pyjamas and a light top on such a winter's day? Did she wonder where she was scurrying to or where she had been?

As she cleaned the Council Chamber steps, Violet was probably the last person to see Mollie Thompson alive, but it would be 10 days before some awful truths about what happened to Mollie were revealed.

Three lost hours

On 11 August 1942 Mary Josephine Thompson, known to one and all as Mollie, disappeared. She just vanished without trace. When Violet saw her, Mollie was just a couple of hundred metres from her 195 Adelaide Street house and heading towards the end of town that was home to the gargantuan water tower that had been built a couple of years earlier. All she had to do was make a right turn, then a left at the next intersection and she was two blocks away from the water tower. But why was she heading in that direction?

So, what happened to the three hours between when Ruby Thompson said her daughter left home at 3am[1]… and Violet Madsen's observations around 6am? And that's just one of the many mysteries in the story of the disappearance of Mollie Thompson… her subsequent death written off as suicide.

Looking back now at the Mollie Thompson drama that developed over 11 days in Maryborough in August 1942, there appears to have been remarkably little interest, and meagre coverage from the local newspaper. Surely this was a page one story to rival the events that were happening in World War II.

A local 24-year-old woman vanished after last being seen in unusual circumstances and it only rated a couple of paragraphs on page two of the paper the next morning. The woman was not named... the article said her parents were anxious as to her safety and welfare. Parents? Mollie's father died 14 years earlier in June 1928. The article contained no quotes from police, no interview with Mollie's mother, Ruby Thompson, and no evidence of any attempt to locate and gather information from anyone who might have seen Mollie.

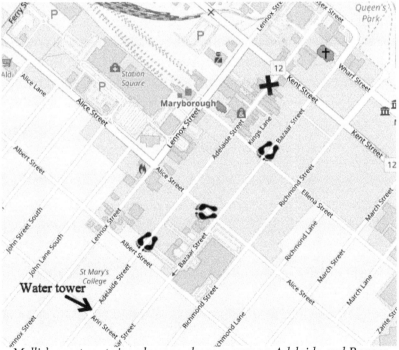

Mollie's exact route is unknown; she was seen on Adelaide and Bazaar Streets, ending up at the water tower. Source: Open Street Map.

A small town and a missing person

Maryborough and surrounds in 1942 still had a population of less than 15,000, and as they say, 'everyone knew everyone… and most of their business.'

The more the locals knew about the facts surrounding Mollie's disappearance, the more likely a memory would be triggered in someone who knew or saw something that might be of vital interest to police.

Surely newspaper coverage would pick up if she wasn't found quickly. Four days after Mollie disappeared her story was still getting just seven lines below the 'personal' column at the bottom of page two.[2] Day five missing, and finally Mollie Thompson was named as the missing person.

Even after ten days Mollie's story was apparently worth just 11 lines in the middle of the second page. There was seldom a mention of Sergeant Fay—her RAAF boyfriend—

Approx. 212 Adelaide Street, Maryborough c1936, close to where Mollie lived at 195 Adelaide Street. Source: State Library of Victoria.

and never a mention of the siblings – two brothers, and three married sisters. But perhaps in a time of heavy media censorship, apparently in the interest of maintaining public morale, we can learn more about what they *didn't* print, rather than what they did.

Meanwhile the search that started out around the centre of Maryborough had now spread over a wide area. The banks of the Mary River were scoured as were the air raid shelters built in case of enemy attack. The town water tower on the corner of Anne and Adelaide Street was inspected on three occasions with no result.

A body is found

And then on Friday 21 August, as police were still patrolling the river, word came that the council plumber, Fred Prickett, who had gone to the top of the massive water tower to fix an indicator that wasn't working, saw Mollie's body in the water.

This was the tower that had been inspected three times over the course of the ten days Mollie had been missing... although we don't know whether that 'inspection' included dragging the bottom or whether it was just someone sticking their head over the top for a look, or something in between.

The tower is 16 metres high and, when it was in use, capable of holding almost four million litres of water. In 1940, when it was built, it was the largest reservoir in Australia and came with some built-in security to prevent unauthorised access. The metal stairs that go to the top of the tower don't go all the way to the ground. They finish almost 12 feet six inches[3] (3.8 metres) short and a ladder is needed to reach the bottom rung.

Above: the water tower where Mollie's body was found. Below: The metal stairs that go to the top of the tower don't go all the way to the ground. They finish about 12 feet six inches[3] (3.8 metres) short and a ladder is needed to reach the bottom rung. Mollie was 5ft 5inches (165cm) tall.

Questions unanswered

Question… and one that remains in many people's minds today: how did a girl who was five feet five inches tall (165cm)[4] gain access to the bottom of the stairs that were at least seven feet (215cm) above her head… well out of reach? Clearly, she would need something to stand on.

And it seems Mollie may have had access. While the regular ladder used by council employees to get to the top of the tower was locked away… another five-foot-high wooden ladder was found at the bottom of the tower. It is mentioned by *The Courier-Mail* and council plumber, Fred Prickett, in his evidence to the Inquest about events on the day Mollie's body was found.

The Courier-Mail reported: "To reach the iron ladder, which begins 10ft. from the ground, the woman must have used a wooden 5ft. ladder, which was found on the ground."

And at the Coronial Inquest Fred's testimony revealed: "The ladder which he had secured to climb to the bottom iron rung was kept locked away in a room under the tank. At the time he got that ladder, there was a shorter ladder lying on the ground immediately under the iron ladder[5]." How did this mystery ladder get there? And Fred went on: "The ladder on the ground was about seven feet in length and to get from it to the bottom rung of the iron ladder a woman would have to exert herself. When she did get hold of the iron ladder she would have to pull herself up by placing her feet against the side of the tank which would be rather difficult."

But there's another and much more curious question: why was that ladder still lying there? Fred found it ten days after Mollie supposedly climbed the tower. Surely if the tower had been inspected three times since Mollie disappeared, the ladder would have been seen and taken as evidence?

Either that or the other possibility is that the wooden ladder wasn't there until the day Fred went to fix the indicator, in which case it probably has no bearing on Mollie's disappearance… which again raises the question of how did she get to the bottom rung?

These were the questions that anecdotal evidence says plenty of Maryborough residents pondered on when they chatted in the street, or over a beer or two in the pub… more than one offered the opinion that Mollie had been murdered, dragged up the stairway and thrown into the reservoir.

A hypothesis

So, in the interest of trying to find a plausible explanation of what happened to Mollie Thompson, let's imagine for a moment that what looks highly unlikely was possible… that Mollie left home in her pyjamas and without shoes at 3am on a winter's morning… or maybe it was closer to 6am if her mother or the newspaper report was mistaken about the time she left. She went somewhere to pick up a seven foot (2.1m) long wooden ladder, carried it to the water tower, managed to get to the top of it to reach the bottom rung of the tower steps and then pulled herself up, climbed to the top and threw herself into the water. Why?

More from the Inquest. A detective Sergeant T. E. Martin told the inquiry: "I found that the girl was in love, she had professed this—with a young man—and owing to different beliefs between her and the man himself, it was considered impossible from her point of view that marriage could take place. Inquiries indicate that this position was in some way responsible for her nervous condition, and her nervous condition was responsible for her death."[6]

And yet also at the inquest, Mollie's mother told the court: "That her daughter had been working at Woolworth's for approximately three years. She had a nervous rash about 12 months previously, but apart from that she had enjoyed good health."

The court also heard from Dr Kenneth Hooper who said: "He saw the girl (Mollie) at her home on August 10 (the day before she disappeared) and questioned then as to the nature of her illness, she told him that for the past couple of months she had not been sleeping well and was worried. From his conversation with her and examination he concluded she was suffering badly from nerves. He prescribed treatment for her. There was nothing about her demeanour which would lead him to believe she might do something rash."[7]

So, Mollie's mother testified that Mollie was normally healthy, was in stable employment and Mollie's doctor said he examined Mollie the day before she disappeared and didn't believe she was likely to do anything rash… in other words… to harm herself.

But clearly something unusual had happened. Mollie was seen by Violet walking down the street in her pyjamas, not far from her home, in the general direction of the water tower… not on the direct route… but veering right into Alice Street and heading that way. Violet didn't see her carrying a ladder, yet the Coroner's eventual verdict must mean she obtained one somewhere and climbed the tower – a difficult proposition according to the council plumber who, presumably, did it regularly. No evidence about who owned the ladder or where it had come from appears to have been offered at the Inquest.

A dangerous love

Mollie was no doubt worried about the relationship she had with a man of different religious beliefs. She had been seeing an air-force sergeant who is mentioned in the inquest and in some newspaper articles. But there seems more to this than just the relationship. *The Truth* newspaper carried a report of a letter she wrote to her mother in which she says she is worried that men stared at her wherever she went… perhaps she was concerned about people's perception of her morals. In the inquest it was revealed by Dr Hooper that: "Later he made a further examination and issued a certificate as to the virtuous life the girl had led, giving it to deceased's mother."[8]

The Government Medical Officer, Dr. J H Bendeich, gave a certificate stating that:

"Death was due to (1) suffocation, (2) drowning. Witness failed to find any bruising, lacerations or abrasions on the body. He was satisfied there were no suspicious circumstances and that the deceased through her nervous conditions was entirely responsible for her own action. It would have been absolutely impossible for anyone to forcibly take the girl up the ladder at the side of the tank. He had found that the girl was in love. She had professed this with a young man but owing to different beliefs between her and the man himself it was considered impossible from her point of view that marriage could take place."[9]

There was no further explanation of the Government Medical Officer's causes of death and so it was that the passing of Mollie Thompson was assigned to the suicide file.

The Coroner found that Mollie had drowned after climbing the Maryborough water tower in the early hours of Tuesday 11 August 1942, and that she was entirely responsible for her own actions.

There was a curious sidebar to this macabre tale. It seems by chance that the good folk of Maryborough were spared the horror that must have reverberated around the town when it was revealed that a body had been decomposing for ten days in the town's drinking water. At the Inquest, Fred Prickett, council plumber was able to reveal that: "Water from the tank ran into the mains in the lower part of the city, and for some days prior to August 11, the water had been shut off. The water in the tank had since been emptied out and the tank refilled."

Life goes on.

How to find Mollie's grave – Monumental FR, Plot 108:

Enter the cemetery off Walker Street, through the gate furthest from the Bruce Highway. Go towards the Mortuary Chapel, when you come to it take the second path to the left (about 100 metres from the gate). Walk down about 60 metres and you will see a large tree on the path. Molly's grave is off to the right and has a wide marker post right beside it with 'Section FR' written on it.

How to find the Maryborough Cemetery at the corner of Walker Street and the Bruce Highway (marked with X):

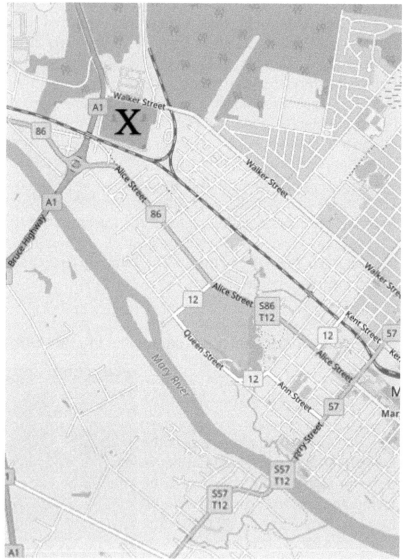

Map:©OpenStreetMap contributors. www.openstreetmap.org

References:

1 M'BRO. POLICE SEEK INFORMATION ABOUT MISSING GIRL (1942, August 12). *Maryborough Chronicle, Wide Bay and Burnett Advertiser* (Qld.: 1860 - 1947), p. 2. Retrieved May 19, 2018, from http://nla.gov.au/nla.news-article151376909

2 NO TRACE OF MISSING GIRL (1942, August 15). *Maryborough Chronicle, Wide Bay and Burnett Advertiser* (Qld.: 1860 - 1947), p. 2. Retrieved May 15, 2018, from http://nla.gov.au/nla.news-article151382572

3 INQUEST INTO YOUNG WOMAN'S TRAGIC DEATH (1942, September 24). *Maryborough Chronicle, Wide Bay and Burnett Advertiser* (Qld.: 1860 - 1947), p. 2. Retrieved June 1, 2018, from http://nla.gov.au/nla.news-article151377818

4 M'BRO. POLICE SEEK INFORMATION ABOUT MISSING GIRL (1942, August 12). Op.cit.

5 INQUEST INTO YOUNG WOMAN'S TRAGIC DEATH (1942, September 24). Op.cit.

6 "I Tried Awful Hard to Be Good" Wrote Dead Girl (1942, October 4). *Truth* (Brisbane, Qld.: 1900 - 1954), p. 18. Retrieved June 1, 2018, from http://nla.gov.au/nla.news-article202383945

7 INQUEST INTO YOUNG WOMAN'S TRAGIC DEATH (1942, September 24). Op.cit.

8 "I Tried Awful Hard to Be Good" Wrote Dead Girl (1942, October 4). Op.cit.

9 INQUEST INTO YOUNG WOMAN'S TRAGIC DEATH (1942, September 24). Op.cit.

Images:

Unidentified (1930). View of Adelaide Street from the fire station tower, Maryborough, 1930. *John Oxley Library, State Library of Queensland.* Retrieved 2 July 2018 from: https://trove.nla.gov.au/version/167839600

Maps: ©OpenStreetMap contributors. www.openstreetmap.org/copyright

Women's work: the ladies of the Criterion Hotel

Dorinda Ann Curtis & Maria Cramp

Interred: Dorinda Ann Curtis (nee Parker), birth date unknown – 19 July 1914 (age at death unknown).

Maria Cramp (formerly Parker, Watt, & nee George), 1836 – 29 September 1875 (aged 39 years).

Location: Dorinda: COE, Section 3, Burial No. 4761.
Maria: COE, Section 4, Burial Number 1002.

Cemetery: South Rockhampton Cemetery, Upper Dawson Road, Allenstown, Rockhampton, QLD 4700.

Dorinda Parker was just a child when her father, Richard, died, leaving her a hotel. The year was 1860, and he must have believed that she would grow up to be ambitious, bright, and could make a go of it. Perhaps she received this for the honour of being the eldest sibling or favourite (Mary Florence was the only other child) or Richard might have wanted to ensure the hotel would stay in the family should his wife remarry. Regardless, history would prove her father made a good decision. So how did the Bush Inn become the Criterion Hotel and remain with the Parker family descendants for decades to come?

Every new town needs a pub

It is well-known that a forming town is usually well served by several good hotels, the railway and a church for repenting on Sunday. In 1856 Rockhampton received its name and the town was officially recognised. In 1857, Dorinda's father, Richard Parker and his business partner George Gannon, established the Bush Inn[1] on the site of where the grand old Criterion Hotel stands today.

Not a glamorous affair by any means – but the iron-bark slab and shingle roof inn welcomed all, including the 15,000 or so gold-seeking hopefuls who passed through town on their way to the newly discovered Canoona goldfields, 60 kilometres to the north of Rockhampton.[2] Richard, his wife, Maria, and their business partner, George, must have been excited by the increase in patronage that the gold brought with it, allowing for renovations to keep the new customers happy. In 1859, the Bush Inn was rebuilt and now boasted a coffee room, garden and billiard room![3]

The gold rush itself was short-lived, but the influx into the town was not. To meet the growing need, other hotels were springing up around town including: the Alliance Hotel in East Street built for botanist Anthelme Thozet (later renowned for his horticultural work); the Rockhampton Hotel built on the river bank in 1859 by John Ward (it burnt down in 1866 and was never rebuilt); the Fitzroy Hotel built c1859–1860 by Charles Wakefield; the Golden Fleece Hotel built by W. James in 1859 at the corner of Quay and William Streets; the Tattersall's Hotel erected in 1860 at the corner of East and Fitzroy Streets, where you will find the Royal Hotel now; the Commercial Hotel on the corner of Little Quay and Denham Streets built in 1861; the Bull and Mouth Hotel in East Street erected in 1863 by George Wilson;[4] and it doesn't stop there… you get the feeling the townsfolk liked a quiet ale or two.

Richard Parker. Source: State Library of Queensland.

Richard departs and the ladies step up

At the Bush Inn's peak in 1860, Richard Parker up and died, leaving Maria *(pictured overleaf)* a young widow with two daughters. As we know, Richard bequeathed the property to Dorinda, his eldest daughter. His business partner, George Gannon, continued in the hotel game, leasing the Commercial Hotel in 1864. But it was Richard's widow, the very capable Maria, 24, who stepped up and kept the Bush Inn going.

A year later, she fortuitously married the principal butcher in town, John Watt, and in 1862 the Bush Inn licence was transferred to a Mr John Ward (not to be confused with her husband, John Watt) and it was renamed the Criterion Hotel.[5] Perhaps in this time, Maria was able to focus on raising her girls and leave the running of the hotel to Mr Ward. But 'Dorinda's' hotel did not stay in the hands of John Ward for long and by the end of the year, the licence was transferred to Thomas Nobbs and The Criterion became even more impressive – it was transformed into a two-storey weatherboard hotel with a veranda fronting Fitzroy Street.[6]

Criterion Hotel ca. 1873. Source: State Library of Queensland.

Maria Cramp (Parker), 1850. From the Capricornia CQ Collection,
CQUniversity Library. Reprinted with their kind permission.

Maria is widowed again

It was not uncommon in the era to be widowed young, and it was Maria's misfortune to find herself in that situation a second time. After only four years of marriage, butcher John Watt died in 1865. John Watt must have taken to Maria's two daughters, as he left the title deeds of some freehold property he possessed to his step-daughters, Dorinda and Mary Florence Parker, in equal shares as tenants in common, or to his married sister should either of the girls die unmarried before the age of 21.[7]

Maria, now 29, married her business manager, John Cramp. When the lease on The Criterion expired the next year, Maria and John took up the licence and returned to run the hotel that was still in the ownership of her daughter, Dorinda.

While managing the hotel, Maria started a new family with John and gave birth to three children. Two sons both died in childhood while living at the hotel: John with debility at one year two months and Joseph with a fever at four months. A daughter, Sarah Ann, lived to the age of six and died from congestion to the lungs – a painfully sad time for the hard-working couple.[8]

Maria was a fiery one, and in 1867, she was "charged with assaulting James Hazlehurst, while in the execution of his public duty as a bailiff in charge of property, in the insolvent estate of John Cramp (defendant's husband.) It appeared that the day after the sale of the Commercial Hotel, Quay Street, defendant was knocking down some shelving and fixtures with an axe. Complainant told her it would do her no good to do, and to leave them for the person who had bought the good-will of the house. She slapped him on the face several times, and subsequently, when he left the bar to give delivery of some beer, she took possession of the bar, and would not let him in."[9] Maria was fined 20 shillings, with 7 shillings costs of Court.

But there was also time for celebrations; Maria's eldest daughter, Dorinda, married George Silas Curtis in 1874. George *(pictured below)*, a businessman and politician, would become a powerful figure around town advocating the separation movement and playing a prominent role in the Rockhampton Chamber of Commerce.

George Silas Curtis. Source: State Library of Queensland.

Meanwhile, Maria along with her husband John, kept the Criterion Hotel going with all its challenges: busy custom, long hours, unruly clientele, multiple events from race meetings to parties, managing staff, dealing with nature such as the 1875 flood which according to the *Morning Bulletin*: "had undermined the river bank so seriously that the whole frontage from the Criterion Hotel upwards was in danger of being carried away."[10]

And of course, death. A number of deaths were recorded at the hotel over the years when Maria and

Dorinda were in management, including that of Mr Samuel Bradford Birkbeck who died in 1867 at the Criterion Hotel after an illness of five days from constipation of the bowels;[11] Mr Thomas Blair who died while at the hotel from the effects of sunstroke in 1869;[12] and Mr Malcolm Turner "who met with fatal injuries by falling from the balcony of the Criterion Hotel"[13] in 1891.

The barmaid, Annie Hoyland, remembered the incident as such: "the deceased had English beer served in a small glass and he drank half of it… the deceased then said 'good night' and left the bar to go to bed… this was about 10 minutes past 12 and the deceased was perfectly sober and sensible; the deceased slept on the top storey [room 28]."[14] His worship declared it an accident and the deceased's brother-in-law, Mr Fraser, agreed.[15] Local ghost storytellers also recall a chambermaid who is rumoured to have taken her own life in room 22 after a broken romance.[16] However, her name remains a mystery and no reporting of the death can be found in the local media.

But death would come to Maria too soon, and in the same year as the flood, she died aged 39; her cause of death listed as heart disease. In her years, Maria Cramp packed in more than many of us will in a lifetime. Her husband, John, continued on in the hotel game, and in 1876 leased the Union Hotel and the Theatre Royal, ordering extensive improvements.[17]

Now a young married woman, Dorinda gathered up the legacy her father had left her and took over the running of the hotel with her husband, George. Their association with the Criterion Hotel would remain for decades, until 1947.[18]

Dorinda Ann Parker, 1870. From the Capricornia CQ Collection, CQUniversity Library. Reprinted with their kind permission.

A woman's touch

Now Dorinda wasn't always on board at the Criterion, as she did stop to have eight children—three sons and five daughters—with George in the 22-year period between 1876 and 1898,[19] and the hotel was leased for a number of years. Of their eight children, two—Dorinda Adela and Herbert John—died in the year of their birth.

In the meantime, the Criterion Hotel was perfectly placed to take advantage of Rockhampton's burgeoning business community and wealth from the gold mine of Mount Morgan.[20] This discovery in the 1880s, just 40km to the west of Rockhampton, put the town on the map. And a facelift for the Criterion was thus in order. Dorinda was lauded for being the lady behind the redesign which saw it transform into a grand three-storey building.[21] The hotel had undergone a few facelifts over the years, but nothing like the transformation that Dorinda delivered – and the new marble, stone and brick dwelling became one of Rockhampton's finest.

Tenders were called for in March 1889 and twelve bids in total were received from as far as Sydney and Brisbane. Dorinda decided on Robert Kirkham of Sydney and accepted his 10,000 pound bid to rebuild her hotel (in today's money that would exceed $1.5 million). No doubt her father, Richard, would have been proud. And so, construction began that year and proceeded for the next twelve months, with a ball marking its official opening on 21 October 1890.[22]

The impressive new Criterion Hotel's main entrance now overlooked the Fitzroy River and was situated on the corner of Quay Street and Fitzroy Street; the old Criterion Hotel building remained on its corner of Quay Lane and Fitzroy Street. It continued to have a life providing the perfect venue for salesmen to display their wares and find a bed for the night. It was later rebuilt for business and shop space.[23]

The Capricornia newspaper reported: "It must be obvious to all, that the new hotel will prove one of the sights of the town. Persons competent to judge declare that north of Sydney there is no better hotel to be found, and the least that can be said is that there are few which excel it in the colonies."[24] A fine tribute to Dorinda.

The Criterion Hotel as it stood in 1930. A far cry from its Bush Inn origns. Source: Queensland State Archives.

Glamour and business at The Criterion

The new Criterion Hotel became renowned for its gala balls and dinner parties and many a celebrity guest graced the venue including: Prince Henry, Duke of Gloucester and his wife Princess Alice; Prime Minister of Australia Sir Robert Menzies; operatic soprano Dame Nellie Melba; cricketer Sir Donald Bradman; and aviator Charles Kingsford Smith. Sporting teams such as the touring English cricket sides have also been accommodated at the hotel.[25]

During the second world war, it was commandeered for the use of American service personnel and served for a period of time as the headquarters of General Robert L. Eichelberger who was on the staff of General Douglas MacArthur. The General was in charge of over 70,000 American troops stationed within the Rockhampton region.[26]

President Roosevelt's wife, Eleanor Roosevelt visited American troops in Rockhampon in 1943. Lieut.-General Eichelberger (front, second from right) was on hand to welcome her. Source: State Library of Queensland.

The Morning Bulletin (Rockhampton) reported that when the General returned to Australia in 1952, his tour was shortened, and "Rockhampton was squeezed out of the itinerary", but he "travelled nearly 1000 miles out of his way to take in a three-hour visit to Rockhampton. The visit, he said, was the highlight of his Australian tour." General Eichelberger said in a broadcast within five minutes of landing: "You have rung in a new bridge on me since I left, but from the air I saw my old home (Yungaba) and the Criterion Hotel."[27]

End of an era

Dorinda died in 1914 (age unknown), and George, her husband, died eight years later in Sydney, aged 79. While his name is marked on the gravestone underneath Dorinda's, there is some confusion around his burial site. Some sources state that George was given full Anglican rites and buried in South Head Cemetery, Sydney.[28] The Waverley Cemetery administration confirms that a George Silas Curtis is there. However, his age is listed at 78, and date of interment as 10 September 1922. On Dorinda's headstone, George is listed as 79 and died 6 October 1922.

All through these years, the Criterion Hotel stayed in the Parker/Curtis family until the last remaining beneficiary of the estate, Ethel (one of Dorinda and George's daughters and granddaughter of Richard Parker), sold the hotel in 1946, when she was aged 67, to Henry Smith. Since then, it continues to rest in the hands of families, with transformations to match the changing needs of the city. Since 1991, Ryan, Megan, and the Turnbull family keep up the tradition.[29]

Today the Criterion Hotel is safely ensconced on the Queensland Heritage Register.

Mary Birch – Critrion Hotel lessee 1903

We'd be remiss not to mention a formidable working woman – Mary Birch. There is little written about Mary, but in the echelons of Rockhampton and Australian history, a more dynamic businesswoman is hard to find. You will know the name Birch; it is synonymous with the Birch Carroll and Coyle cinemas, and George H. Birch, Mary's husband also leased or managed a number of hotels including the Grand Hotel in Emu Park from 1887-92; the Comley's Hotel in Emu Park in 1892; the Union Hotel in Rockhampton in 1892; and Dorinda's Criterion Hotel from 1903.[30]

Mary and George lived in the suburb The Range on the corner of Queen and James Street and had two daughters Meta and Mary Dorothy. Mary Birch was widowed aged 57 years in 1917 and stepped up to continue her husband's extensive business activities including running their hotels. While the Birch, Carroll and Coyle Company wasn't formed until 1923, Earl's Court Theatre at Rockhampton was owned by the Birch family – who operated this and other theatres in the town from 1910 onwards with major renovations taking place in the 1930s. Eventually, Earl's Court would be incorporated into the then Birch Carroll partnership.[31]

Australian Variety Theatre wrote: "The inclusion of the Birch name in the formation of Birch, Carroll and Coyle Ltd in 1923 was therefore as much an acknowledgement of her [Mary's] involvement in the continued success of the Birch-Carroll firm as her husband's."[32] There are volumes that could be written about the work of Mary in the development of Rockhampton's arts and theatre industry, but for a brief moment, she crossed paths with Dorinda and

Maria while leasing the Criterion Hotel in 1903, and helped keep the home and business fires burning.

Mary died on 23 December 1956, aged 96 years.

You can find the grave of Mary Ann Agnes Birch (nee Cannon) in the **Roman Catholic, Sec 8, Row 2, Grave No 8** of the North Rockhampton Cemetery, Yaamba Road (cnr Moores Creek Road). The entrance to North Rockhampton cemetery is off the Bruce Highway. Once you have entered go past the cemetery buildings on your left and through four roadway intersections. You will find Compartment 8 immediately on your right and Section two is actually Row 2. Mary's grave is the second last in that row as you travel away from the entrance.

The Criterion Hotel is open for business if you wish to raise a glass in honour of the Criterion's working women.

Above: The Criterion Hotel today with the 'Bush Inn' bar at the side.

How to find Dorinda Curtis' and Maria Cramp's graves in South Rockhampton Cemetery at:

- Dorinda: COE, Section 3, Burial No. 4761;
- Maria: COE, Section 4, Burial Number 1002.

Both these ladies are in the Church of England section of South Rockhampton cemetery and are not hard to find. Their graves lie side by side near an entrance to the cemetery opposite number 39 Ferguson Street. Enter through that gate and immediately turn right, walk down about 20 metres and you will find the ladies just a few metres from the fence in the shade of a large Norfolk Pine.

How to find South Rockhampton Cemetery:

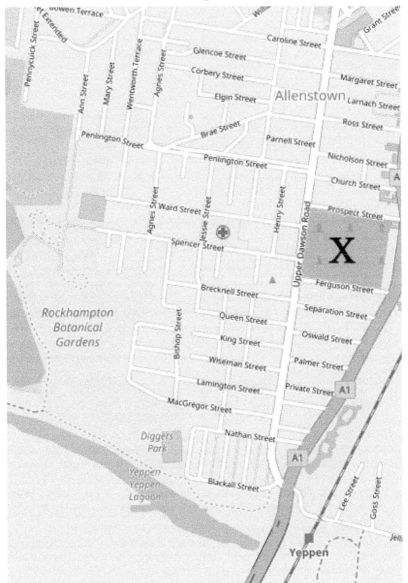

Map:©OpenStreetMap contributors. www.openstreetmap.org

References:

1 Wikipedia contributors. (2 June 2018). Criterion Hotel, Rockhampton. In *Wikipedia*. Retrieved 22 June 2018 from URL: https://en.wikipedia.org/w/index. php?title=Criterion_Hotel,_Rockhampton&oldid=844086086

2 McKenzie, Kirsty, Grand Old Dame, *R.M. Williams Outback Magazine*, Issue #84, Aug/Sep 2012. Retrieved 30 June 2018 from URL: https://www. outbackmag.com.au/grand-old-dame/

3 Wikipedia contributors. (2 June 2018). Criterion Hotel. Op.cit.

4 Bird, J. T., S. *The Early History of Rockhampton, dealing chiefly with events up till 1870.* Retrieved 29 June 2018 from URL: http://www.textqueensland.com.au/item/book/f05857c88c74d62aece433d5c9ae0a74

5 & 6 Wikipedia contributors. (2 June 2018). Criterion Hotel. Op.cit.

7 The Courts. (21 Nov 1868). *The Queenslander* (Brisbane, Qld.: 1866 - 1939), p6. Retrieved 1 July 2018, from http://nla.gov.au/nla.news-article20321597

8 (Family Notices 22 Feb 1871). *Northern Argus* (Rockhampton: 1865-1874), p3. Retrieved 22 June 2018 from: http://nla.gov.au/nla.news-article216806306)

9 POLICE COURT—ROCKHAMPTON. (1867, April 20). *Rockhampton Bulletin and Central Queensland Advertiser* (Qld: 1861 - 1871), p3. Retrieved 1 July 2018 from http://nla.gov.au/nla.news-article51566352

10 The Morning Bulletin, ROCKHAMPTON. (1 Mar 1878). *Morning Bulletin* (Qld: 1878-1954), p2. Retrieved 1 July 2018 from http://nla.gov.au/nla.news-article52396732

11 SYDNEY. (6 June 1867). *Rockhampton Bulletin and Central Queensland Advertiser* (1861-1871), p2. Retrieved 1 July 2018, http://nla.gov.au/nla.news-article51565106

12 SYDNEY. (16 Jan 1869). *Rockhampton Bulletin and Central Queensland Advertiser* (Qld: 1861-1871), p2. Retrieved 1 July 2018 from http://nla.gov.au/nla.news-article51574892

13 THE FATAL ACCIDENT AT THE CRITERION HOTEL. (11 March 1891). *Morning Bulletin* (Rockhampton, Qld: 1878 - 1954), p5. Retrieved 1 July 2018, from http://nla.gov.au/nla.news-article52343048

14 & 15. Ibid.

16 Casey, Anna, *Rockhampton heritage buildings virtual tour of Quay Street*, 16 May, 2013. Retrieved 30 June 2018 from URL: https://www.slideshare.net/goannagoanna08/rockhampton-heritage-buildings-virtual-tour-of-quay-street

17 OLD PROGRAMMES (17 Feb 1934). *Morning Bulletin* (Qld.: 1878 - 1954), p. 3. Retrieved 30 June 2018, from http://nla.gov.au/nla.news-article55525706

18 Wikipedia contributors. (2 June 2018). Criterion Hotel. Op.cit.

19 McDonald, Lorna. L., 'Curtis, George Silas (1845–1922)', *Australian Dictionary of Biography*, National Centre of Biography, ANU. Retrieved 29 June 2018, http://adb.anu.edu.au/biography/curtis-george-silas-5855/text9955

20 Wikipedia contributors. (2 June 2018). Criterion Hotel. Op.cit.

21 Bird, J. T., S. Op.cit.

22 & 23 Wikipedia contributors. (2018, June 2). Criterion Hotel. Op.cit.

24 THE NEW CRITERION HOTEL. (30 Aug 1890). *The Capricornian* (Qld: 1875-1929), p22. Retrieved 30 June 2018, from http://nla.gov.au/nla.news-article67952276

25 & 26 Wikipedia contributors. (2018, June 2). Criterion Hotel. Op.cit.

27 EICHELBERGER TELLS US HIGHLIGHT OF TOUR TO COME BACK HERE (2 May 1952). *Morning Bulletin* (Rockhampton, Qld: 1878-1954), p1. Retrieved 30 June 2018, from http://nla.gov.au/nla.news-article57099576

28 McDonald, Lorna. L., 'Curtis, George Silas (1845–1922)'. Op.cit.

29 Hotel History, *The Criterion*, 2016. Retrieved 30 June 2018: http://thecriterion.com.au/

30 Birch Carroll & Coyle, Organisations & Partnerships [A-L], *Australian Variety Theatre Archive*, Popular Culture Entertainment: 1850-1930, 2 April 2011. Retrieved 19 June 2018 from URL: https://ozvta.com/organisations-a-l/

31 Cryle, Denis and Johansen, Grace, *Maintaining a Tradition of Mixed Entertainments: Birch, Carroll and Coyle's regional Queensland Wintergarden Theatres, Screening the Past*, 13 Mar 2006. Retrieved 19 June 2018, https://bit.ly/2m0TRVy

32 Birch Carroll & Coyle, Organisations & Partnerships [A-L], Australian Variety Theatre Archive. Op.cit.

Images:

Central Queensland University Library. *Capricornia Central Queensland Collection* (1870). [Mrs George Silas Curtis (nee Dorinda Ann Parker)]. Reprinted with kind permission of the Central Queensland University Library.

Central Queensland University. Library. *Capricornia Central Queensland Collection* (1850). [Maria Parker (Mrs Richard Parker)]. Reprinted with the kind permission of the Central Queensland University Library.

Unidentified (1873). Criterion Hotel in Rockhampton, ca. 1873. *John Oxley Library, State Library of Queensland*. Retrieved 19 June 2018 from URL: https://trove.nla.gov.au/version/167835269

Criterion Hotel - Rockhampton, 1930 - 1959. *Queensland State Archives*. Retrieved 19 June 2018 from URL: https://trove.nla.gov.au/version/252859244

- Unidentified Richard Parker. *John Oxley Library, State Library of Queensland*. Retrieved 19 June 2018 from URL: https://trove.nla.gov.au/version/47916699

- Unidentified Hon. George Silas Curtis, 1845-1922. *John Oxley Library, State Library of Queensland*. Retrieved 22 June 2018 from URL: https://trove.nla.gov.au/version/167815692

Eleanor Roosevelt Arriving in Rockhampton, Queensland, 9 September 1943. (2007). *John Oxley Library, State Library of Queensland*. Retrieved 1 July 2018 from URL: https://hdl.handle.net/10462/deriv/90065

Maps: ©OpenStreetMap contributors. www.openstreetmap.org/copyright

Murder most foul
The Thomas Griffin story

Interred: Constable John Francis Power, 1840 – 6 Nov 1867 (aged 27 years).
Constable Patrick William Cahill, 1842 – 6 Nov 1867 (aged 25 years).

Location: There are two sets of graves for Constables Power and Cahill:

- An obelisk for Constables Power and Cahill is just inside the Prospect Street gates, compartment Roman Catholic, approximately Row 3 and inside the gate by about 20 metres (this bears no relation to where they are buried. See description and map at end of story);

- A second memorial placed by the Queensland Police Service in July 2013 is in compartment Roman Catholic, Section 9. Constable Power is in 384, Constable Cahill is in 385. This is in the correct row where the men are believed to be buried but is probably not where they are actually buried.

Cemetery: South Rockhampton Cemetery, Upper Dawson Road, Allenstown, QLD 4700.

Thomas John Augustus Griffin, Assistant Gold Commissioner. Source: State Library of Queensland.

There were many 'firsts' when Queensland became a state, separating from New South Wales in 1859. The celebrations started when Queen Victoria signed the paperwork on 6 June and were still ongoing the actual day of separation 10 December. Everything was new. George Bowen was the first Governor; the first elections were held in 1860; and Robert George Wyndham Herbert became the first Premier. We had a new government and a new police force and with that, inevitably, the first Queensland police murders; two officers shockingly killed by a man who was one of their own.[1]

The first murderer of Queensland police was Thomas John Griffin. He was not some opportunistic bushranger who preyed on miners heading to and from the various gold rushes in central Queensland, instead, he was a man who held a position most would associate with trust, honesty and decency. He should have been far from the treacherous, calculating, cold-blooded killer which in reality he was, seemingly fully deserving of the fate which eventually claimed him.

In the 1860s Central Queensland was abuzz with activity as gold-seekers from all around the world set their sights on the riches that were there for the taking. The first rush had occurred when the area was still part of New South Wales, in 1858 at Canoona… about 50 kilometres from the major settlement in the area, Rockhampton. It only lasted six months, but gold valued at around 180,000 pounds was unearthed in that time.

Three years later in 1861 the rush was on to Peak Downs and within two years there were more than a thousand men on the field, and nearby Clermont became a flourishing town even if most of it was still under canvas. It also became the place where miners who had found gold could have it exchanged for cash. The service was provided by the Queensland Police which escorted gold from Clermont to Rockhampton and currency back to the tented town.

The hunter and the hunted

To understand how Thomas Griffin and his victims, Queensland Police Troopers John Power and Patrick Cahill, became the hunter and the hunted in November of 1867, we need to learn something of Griffin's earlier life.

By anyone's standards, Griffin's service life as a soldier and a policeman appeared to be exemplary. And he carried it well. He was described by someone who knew him as being tall and of military bearing with a long fair beard and hard, cruel blue eyes.[2]

He joined the Irish Constabulary at a fairly young age and then served with some distinction in the Crimea. Police who volunteered for that conflict were given free passage to Australia at its conclusion… an offer that Griffin took up... arriving in Melbourne late in 1856.

And it was here that the rogue in Griffin began to assert itself. He married a woman by the name of Crosby and after disposing of her limited wealth, decided to throw her off his trail. He fled to New Zealand (or Tasmania) and arranged for his death notice to be published in a local paper and a copy forwarded to his wife.

With his deception successful he was free to return, and he went to Sydney where he obtained a position with the New South Wales Police. This began a chain of positions, none of which bore any weight in the considerations that would lead him to kill two men… until in 1863 when he found himself holding the positions of Gold Commissioner and Police Magistrate at Clermont, which was still very much a pioneer tented town.

It was a rough and ready place and in need of someone who could be tough but fair. Griffin appeared to be just the man for the job.

The Gold Escort group L-R seated: **Constable Patrick William Cahill, Constable John Francis Power and Gold Commissioner Thomas John Griffin.** *The two Mounted Police officers standing at the back are not named. Source: Queensland Police Museum.*

A dangerous man for the job

Before long everyone knew the name Thomas Griffin. In the four years he had in Clermont he became widely known… but not necessarily universally liked. He, of course, had his own close circle of friends, but outside that clique, his harsh and often unjust rulings from the bench and his domineering and oppressive behaviour soon left him highly unpopular. Eventually, a public petition to the government saw Griffin removed and sent to Rockhampton as assistant Gold Commissioner. He'd been tough… but not fair.

But when Griffin left Clermont he took with him something that may have been part of his make-up when he arrived there, but was now prominent and dangerous – his addiction to gambling. It was said that he visited a house in Clermont where heavy gambling was carried out in a room isolated from other parts of the building. According to some, his losses at this place were 'great'.[3]

In all likelihood it was that which drove the next episode in this terrible tale. It seems some months before his removal from Clermont, Griffin had been entrusted with some gold and cash by six Chinese men to send to Rockhampton by escort. We don't know what happened to it… and neither did the Chinese. When they found out he was in Rockhampton, they constantly sought some account of what had happened to the gold and money but time after time Griffin put them off with some excuse or another.

Finally he arranged a meeting with the men for the morning of 30 October, where he paid out the full amount owing, 252 pounds, in six rolls of one-pound notes, each with his handwriting on the outside of the roll. So where did the money come from? If Griffin had it all the time, there was no need to continually defer the Chinese and if he was then able to suddenly pay up, what is important about the timing of that?

Griffin had arrived in Rockhampton on 19 October, two days after the most recent shipment of gold taken by escort from Clermont. It was some 2806 ounces of gold taken down by a Sergeant Julian and his two troopers, Power and Cahill.

When Griffin arrived in town he had mentioned to Sergeant Julian that he might send him, Julian, back to Clermont with the cash, and on Friday 25 October he gave instructions to Julian to collect the money the next morning from the bank… which he did on the Saturday… some 8151 pounds.

A crime plays out

Next came the most farcical episode in this unfolding drama. There were two attempts to begin the journey from Rockhampton to Clermont, and on both occasions, the money ended up back in the bank.

Griffin managed to manipulate the situation so that on 29 October he was able to suspend Sergeant Julian, who was suspicious about Griffin's intentions. This eventually left Power in charge of the money—now reduced to four thousand pounds—and Griffin said he would take care of it for him so he could get a good night's sleep… and took the cash away from their camp.

The next day, 30 October, the day after Griffin got his hands on the money, was pay day for the Chinese men and as we know, they were duly recompensed for their missing money and gold.

Now it also seems that Power did not trust Griffin... and with good reason. The money was in Power's care... he was responsible for it and when Griffin handed the package back to him the next day he wanted to make sure it was all there. He asked for the outside cover to be removed so he could check. Griffin, however, said: "Oh I assure you it's alright; it has not been out of my possession since you gave it to me."[4]

Power didn't say anything more but was able to feel, as he placed the money package into a saddle bag, that there was a space that should have been filled by a wad of notes. A little later he asked Griffin to seal the bags containing the money, including the bag that was short one wad, with his, Griffin's, seal. Knowing that Power would refuse to take charge of the money if he didn't, Griffin applied his seal to the bags... and in doing so ensured the fate of Cahill, Power and himself. Once the bags were opened in Clermont and the money found missing, if the seals were unbroken, suspicion would fall on Griffin, as he had taken the money bag away by himself.

After what amounted to a week of delays, the escort finally set out on 1 November. It consisted of Assistant Gold Commissioner Thomas Griffin, Trooper John Francis Power who was in charge of the cash—somewhere around four thousand pounds—and Trooper Patrick William Cahill. Cahill and Power carried revolvers. At the time it was thought that Griffin was unarmed, an incorrect assumption as events would reveal.

A treacherous act

While the Assistant Gold Commissioner had declared his intention to travel only a short distance with the escort, in reality what he meant was he would only go as far as was needed to achieve his treachery. It was probably the alertness of Power and Cahill that extended the trip for as far as it lasted. But in his book, *The Early History of Rockhampton*, J.T.S. Bird queries what may have happened along the way. He reports:

"There are no means of accurately knowing what took place on the journey, but Griffin, it is believed, made more than one attempt to kill the men before he actually did it. He rode behind them, and at one time shot at Power through the case of the revolver, the ball going through Power's coat. Of course, Griffin explained the weapon had gone off accidentally." [5]

The luckiest man in this sordid tale now enters the picture. He was Constable Moynihan who met up with the escort while he was out looking for run-away police horses. Power saw this as his chance to rid himself of Griffin and without telling Moynihan why, asked him if he would accompany himself and Cahill to Clermont to save Mr Griffin the trouble.

Griffin appeared to agree with the idea, telling Moynihan that the escort would have to leave their campsite early the next morning. Before Moynihan and the escort turned in for the night, Griffin asked Moynihan if he would have a drink. Moynihan said he would have a brandy, which Griffin fetched for him and then went to bed. The brandy must have been drugged because Moynihan did not wake until 10 am… four hours after the escort had hit the road with Griffin still in charge.

Early in the day on 5 November, the escort arrived at the Mackenzie River and the nearby Bedford Hotel. They all had breakfast at the Hotel and set up camp. Griffin said he would travel back to Rockhampton with hotel owner Mr Bedford the next morning. Power and Cahill would also leave in the early hours of 6 November. They left the hotel at about 8.30pm after having drunk a couple of bottles of beer. Griffin followed shortly after, taking a bottle of brandy with him.

Bedford also went to bed but his sleep was disturbed twice during the night… by gunshots. He heard two; the first woke him at about 2am… and another about an hour and a half later. Half an hour after the second shot Griffin arrived ready to set off on the trip back to Rockhampton. Griffin apparently looked tired. Bedford inquired of the shots and Griffin said Power had gone out to look for the horses and got lost. He fired a shot to attract attention. Griffin said that was the only shot he heard.

So, Bedford and Griffin set out with Bedford, leaving a married couple, Mr and Mrs Petersen, in charge of the Hotel. When the escort arrived the day before, Mrs Petersen lent the men a billy and after Bedford departed she went to Power and Cahill's camp to get it back. As she saw what looked like one of the men asleep in his blankets she called out. Receiving no reply, she went back to the hotel where she told her husband the troopers were sound asleep in their camp.

That afternoon the Petersens told a visitor to the hotel about the troopers being still in their camp and he suggested they leave them alone as they may have been lying in ambush or on the lookout for some wanted person.

A gruesome discovery

There was no movement from the camp that day and the next afternoon when he was out looking for horses, Mr Petersen noticed a strong smell coming from the camp and went to investigate. He found Power and Cahill lying dead within a few feet of each other.

A stockman from a nearby station was sent to the Native Police barracks on the Mackenzie River and by day's end Acting Sub-Inspector Stokes had been to the camp to confirm the report, and the officer-in-charge of the barracks, Sub-Inspector Uhr thoroughly inspected the area and rode to Gainsford to report the matter. Most notably, the package of one-pound notes was gone and the wrapper in which it had been housed was found partially burned in the camp fire. Constable Moynihan, who previously encountered the escort on the road, was sent to Rockhampton with the gruesome news.

In the meantime, Bedford and Griffin had arrived back in Rockhampton on Thursday 7 November, having completed the final 46 kilometres or so by train from Westwood. Shortly after leaving Bedford's Hotel, Griffin had left the road and gone 30 or 40 yards into the bush… presumably to answer a call of nature. It must have been a popular place because later on the same day a fellow by the name of Thomas Pitt found a one-pound note which was later shown to be from the money Griffin stole from Power when he 'minded' the cash for him.

Now just an aside for one moment: the reason the note was able to be identified, along with others, is because the shipment of cash had been 'narrated'… the nineteenth-century term for 'marked', so it could be identified later. It would be staggering if Griffin did not know this. Even if he did know but believed he would be able to take all the marked money out of circulation after paying the Chinese men and killing the escort constables, his carelessness in disposing of the notes is equally staggering.

Again, the day after Bedford and Griffin arrived in Rockhampton they and another man, Hornby, stopped in at the Commercial Hotel in Quay Street for a drink and Griffin paid for their beverages with a note that was not only marked and part of the proceeds of a double murder... but was particularly damaged. In fact, it was so torn that the barmaid didn't want to accept it. It was finally taken but because it was so tattered was put aside at the bank where it attracted attention. Attention that eventually revealed it was one of the notes taken away by Constable Power as part of the escort parcel.

Incriminating himself

Griffin continued to incriminate himself as events unfolded. When Sub-Inspector Urh first examined the murder scene, probably because of the decomposing nature of the bodies, he arrived at the conclusion that Power and Cahill had been poisoned, and that was the story that rapidly circulated around Central Queensland and in Rockhampton.

On Saturday 9 November a party of senior police, including Griffin and Sub-Inspector Elliott, a detective and a doctor, was due to leave by train for Westwood and on to the murder scene. Before they left, Griffin had a conversation with a Mr T.S. Hall who asked Griffin, "However did those two fellows get the poison? Griffin replied, they are not poisoned: it's all a trumped-up yarn – a false report; they are shot and you will see if they are not." [6] Remember, there had been no suggestion by anyone up to this point that the escort policemen had died from anything but poisoning.

By now suspicion was falling on Griffin. Sub-Inspector Elliott had a conversation with him in which he suggested all types of theories about how the men might have died and concluded that Griffin had no idea he was suspected.

On the way to the campsite the party stopped at a wayside inn. After dinner, Elliott, who had become convinced of Griffin's involvement in the murders, took the inn-keeper aside and set up a plan to make the eventual apprehension of Griffin somewhat safer for all involved. He told the inn-keeper he and Griffin would need a private room to have a drink and talk about what had happened and what should happen next. He instructed the man to serve Griffin whatever he wanted and that he, Elliott, would always ask for a gin… and he was to be given water. His plan worked and given the November heat, a long day's ride and several drinks, it wasn't long before Griffin was sound asleep.

Once the snores of Griffin were constant, Elliot relieved him of his revolver and made it inoperable by scraping the detonating powder off the firing caps and dampening them with water. It was a fine plan and only threatened to backfire on Elliot once, when a black snake decided to cross the road in front of the party. Ever one keen to demonstrate his skills with a revolver, Griffin whipped his weapon from its holster and was about to fire when Elliot yelled out, "For God's sake don't shoot Griffin; this brute I am riding will not stand fire and will put me off." [7] Griffin put his gun away, the day was saved and Elliott killed the snake with a stick.

When the party arrived at Bedford's Hotel the doctor examined the bodies of Power and Cahill, which had been exhumed after being temporarily buried by the native police. The doctor reported to Sub-Inspector Elliot after his examination and told him he had found both men had bullet wounds to the head. Elliot told him not to mention that to anyone else. The doctor would later say he could not be sure whether both men died from those wounds or were previously poisoned.

After a short conversation with the detective who was part of the party, Elliot and the detective arrested Griffin with Elliott saying: "I arrest you on suspicion of having murdered John Power and Patrick Cahill."[8] The news travelled fast, reaching Rockhampton within two days. Rockhampton newspaper reports said that the arrest of Griffin caused: "widespread excitement" and that a great crowd assembled at the Rockhampton railway station to meet Griffin, but he was taken out at Yeppen, just on the outskirts of town, and taken to the lockup in a cab.[9]

Griffin's trial for the murder of his police colleagues began in Rockhampton on 18 March 1868 before Judge Lutwyche and a jury. The evidence, much of which has been outlined here, was overwhelming. Some of the most damning came from the Chinese men who had been stopped in Sydney just as they were about to board a ship bound for their native country. It was shown that the notes with which they were reimbursed by Griffin were from the marked batch taken from the bank by Power. The bank manager, who had also known Griffin in Clermont, swore the writing on the outside of the rolls of notes belonged to the accused.

There were more than 60 witnesses for the prosecution;

for the defence, just one. On 25 March at ten minutes past three, the jury retired. It returned one hour and two minutes later with a verdict of guilty. Griffin was asked if there was any reason why he should not be sentenced to death and poured out a long and rambling statement.

After Griffin's statement, Judge Lutwyche, having donned the black cap, was reported by the *Sydney Morning Herald* as saying;

"Thomas John Griffin you have been found guilty by a jury of your countrymen of the crime of wilful murder and I can say that sitting in my place here, I never heard circumstantial evidence of guilt more satisfactory or more conclusive. I will add little to give you more pain. My own feelings are deep and painful enough when I see you in the position, convicted of a crime unparalleled in the annals of Australian history. I am unequal to the task of expressing the pain the anguish and the horror I feel. I'll only do what the law compels me, that is to pass a sentence, and that is, that you Thomas John Griffin be taken from the place where you stand to the place from whence you came, and there, at such time that may be appointed by the acting Governor, with the advice of the Executive Council, be hanged by the neck until you are dead; and may God, in His infinite mercy have mercy upon your soul.' The venerable judge was deeply affected at the conclusion of the address and was overcome by emotion. The prisoner also seemed affected, but left the court in charge of the police with composure."[10]

And so it was that on 1 June 1868 on gallows which had been built within the hearing and possibly the sight of the imprisoned Thomas Griffin, he was executed. The killer of John Power and Patrick Cahill was the first man to be hanged in Rockhampton Jail.

Vandals at the grave

But there is more to tell in this terrible tale. After the execution of Griffin, his body was buried in the Church of England section of what is now called the South Rockhampton Cemetery. In those days it was the only one in the city. Apparently, according to the *Queenslander* newspaper on 20 June 1868, the sexton, a fellow named Tucker had a tip-off that someone would attempt to rob Griffin's grave.

At the same time, the body of a man who had died after arriving in Rockhampton on board the steamer *Tinonee,* which plied the Queensland coast, arrived at the cemetery for burial. The sexton, Tucker, thought to thwart any attempt to disturb Griffin's grave he would bury the unnamed new arrival on top of Griffin's coffin. Despite this, grave robbers managed to extract Griffin's coffin and steal his head. Macabre but true. According to the newspaper article, the operators of Chambers of Horrors would pay up to fifty pounds for such an item and was outraged when the government only offered twenty pounds reward for its return: "It is a disgrace to the Government that the reward they offer for the detection of the crime is not more than they would offer for a good horse or bullock".[11]

Despite the reward, stories abounded in Rockhampton for many years that the head was buried in a 'public spot', removed again surreptitiously and re-buried in a front garden of a house just a little way out of town, where it remained for many years. Its location, if it still exists, is now a mystery.

And where was the money that Griffin had stolen from the escort troopers? He had wrapped it in a blanket secured by six straps and hidden it in a hollow tree. While he was in jail awaiting execution, Griffin tried to talk his turnkeys... his prison guards... into letting him free if he revealed the location of the cash. Griffin gave two of them, John Lee and Alfred Grant, sketches of the location and they made three attempts to find the plunder but failed each time.

After the execution of Griffin, the turkeys told the authorities about Griffin's attempt at a bribe. The money was tracked down fairly quickly and found to be all there, less the money given to the Chinese men and eighteen pounds which Griffin spent or lost. Lee and Grant were dismissed from government service for their dishonesty but did get a 200-pound reward for delivering information about where the proceeds of the murders could be found.

Grave questions

One curiosity remains from this whole sordid affair; why did the funeral of John Power and Patrick Cahill not take place until more than 18 months after their murder... and why are there two sets of graves for them in the South Rockhampton Cemetery? The best explanation that can be obtained is that the bodies of the troopers remained buried out by the Mackenzie River crossing, where the men were killed, until such time as the money was raised by public subscription for their memorial. Then on 15 July 1869, once the tall sandstone monument with its cross on the top was in place, the funeral went ahead.

The *Northern Argus* reported on the turn-out: "The remains of the unfortunate troopers Power and Cahill were followed to the cemetery on Thursday by the larger portion of the inhabitants of Rockhampton; many hundreds in traps and on horse back and a long concourse of people on foot lined the footpaths and swelled the procession to the gates of the burial ground."[12]

As for why there are two sets of graves for Power and Cahill, again it seems that for convenience at the time, many of the memorials in that cemetery lie along the central north-south pathway and not necessarily where the people they commemorate are buried. In 1869 the Power/Cahill obelisk would have been particularly prominent; just inside the Prospect Street gates, probably not surrounded by the headstones we see there today and therefore easy to find.

Closer to the actual burial place of the two men is the second memorial in the cemetery which was placed there by the Queensland Police Service in July 2013 *(pictured overleaf)*. It is in the row indicated on the cemetery layout… but not necessarily exactly where the men are buried.

The story of Power and Cahill has always been important in Rockhampton… it's never been forgotten. When, back in 1910, the men's cemetery monument had fallen into disrepair, a local councillor, Alderman McClelland, wrote a letter to the paper under the name 'Drummer Boy' suggesting more public subscription should be encouraged to repair the stone. The money was raised and the monument repaired. The local paper concluded its story by reminding readers that the men had been given a military funeral... and the drummer boy that day had been Alderman McClelland.[13]

The memorial erected in South Rockhampton Cemetery by the Queensland Police Service.

How to find the gravesites of Constables John Power and Patrick Cahill:

To find South Rockhampton Cemetery, refer to the map on page 133. To find the graves and memorial of Constables John Power and Patrick Cahill, as listed at the front of this chapter, there are two locations in South Rockhampton Cemetery: one where they were believed to have been buried, and a second nearer to where it has been revealed they are in fact interred. The locations are not far from each other.

Enter the cemetery from Upper Dawson Road almost immediately opposite the school and next to the car park. Travel down the grass track about 150 metres and you will come to a track intersection. Turn left, go past the large map of the cemetery and in about 75 metres you will come to a sign indicating the Roman Catholic section. Go past that sign and you will find the original burial place of Power and Cahill on your right, just before you reach the fence.

The second location is down the hill and to the right of the first. The row numbering system is hard to apply here as extra rows have been added between the numbered rows over the years. The easiest way to find the location of where Power and Cahill are buried is to walk at a 45-degree angle to the fence toward the centre of the Catholic section and in 60 metres or so you will be in the vicinity of the grave. It looks comparatively new and has two bronze plaques on it.

References:

1 ROLL OF HONOUR 1867 – 1883, *Queensland Police*, 2 December 2015. Retrieved 6 July 2018 from URL: https://www.police.qld.gov.au/aboutUs/commemoration/honour/roll.htm

2 Hill, W.R.O., *45 Years Experiences in North Queensland 1861 to 1905*, Brisbane: H. POLE & CO., PRINTERS, 1907. Retrieved 10 July 2018 from URL: https://espace.library.uq.edu.au/view/.../AU4024_45_Years_in_North_Queensland.pdf

3 - 9 Bird, J.T.S., *The Early History of Rockhampton, dealing chiefly with events up till 1870*. Printed and Published by the Morning Bulletin, 1904. Retrieved online 10 July 2018 from URL: https://espace.library.uq.edu.au/view/UQ:216457/AU4009_Rockhampton.pdf&bookreader=true#page/1/mode/1up

10 THE MACKENZIE MURDERS. (1868, April 6). *The Sydney Morning Herald* (NSW: 1842 - 1954), p. 3. Retrieved July 2, 2018, from http://nla.gov.au/nla.news-article13164275

11 DESECRATION OF GRIFFIN'S GRAVE. (1868, June 20). *The Queenslander* (Brisbane, Qld.: 1866 - 1939), p. 8. Retrieved July 3, 2018, from http://nla.gov.au/nla.news-article20319169

12 THU PUBLIC FUNERAL OF MESSES. POWER AND CAHILL. (1869, July 17). *Northern Argus* (Rockhampton, Qld.: 1865 - 1874), p. 2. Retrieved July 3, 2018, from http://nla.gov.au/nla.news-article214284186

13 The Griffin Murder. (1910, August 11). *Gympie Times and Mary River Mining Gazette* (Qld.: 1868 - 1919), p. 4. Retrieved July 3, 2018, from http://nla.gov.au/nla.news-article187670761

Images:

Unidentified Thomas John Augustus Griffin. *John Oxley Library, State Library of Queensland.* Retrieved 13 January 2018 from URL: https://trove.nla.gov.au/version/167819243

(1867). Gold Escort group. *Queensland Police Museum.* Reproduced with the kind permission of the Queensland Police Museum. Retrieved 10 July 2018 from URL: https://trove.nla.gov.au/version/216543649

Newsclipping below: THE MACKENZIE MURDERS. (1868, April 6). *The Sydney Morning Herald* (NSW : 1842 - 1954), p. 2. Retrieved July 10, 2018, from http://nla.gov.au/nla.news-article13164275

MACKENZIE MURDERS.

THE trial of Thomas John Griffin for the murder of troopers Power and Cahill at the Mackenzie River was commenced at Rockhampton, on the 18th March, and lasted to the 25th. Sixty witnesses were called for the Crown, and the evidence occupies several pages of the local journals.

ROCKHAMPTON ASSIZES.

WEDNESDAY, MARCH 18.

Before his Honor Judge Lutwyche and a common jury.

MURDER.

Thomas John Griffin, under remand, stood indicted for that he, on the 6th day of November, 1867, at the Mackenzie River, did feloniously, wilfully, and with malice aforethought, kill and murder one John Power and one Patrick Cahill.

Prisoner pleaded " Not Guilty."

In Loving Memory of
Our dear
Mother SARAH WELCH 38 years
Sister LUCY WELCH 3 years
Brother CHARLES WELCH 3 months
Drowned cyclone 21-1-1918
Father PETER WELCH 73 years
Passed away 18-5-1939
In God's Care

In Loving Memory of
Our dear sisters
ELIZABETH WELCH 14 years
ROSE WELCH 9 years
MABEL WELCH 6 years
Drowned cyclone 21-1-1918

In God's Care

The cyclone with no name
The Welch family

Interred:

Sarah Welch, approx. 1880 – 21 January 1918 (aged 38 years).

Lucy Welch, 10 June 1914 – 21 January 1918(aged 3 years).

Charles Welch, 18 October 1917 – 21 January 1918 (aged 3 mths).

Elizabeth Welch, 16 August 1903 – 21 January 1918 (aged 14 years).

Rose Welch, 14 July 1908 – 21 January 1918 (aged 9 years).

Mabel Welch, 3 October 1911 – 21 January 1918 (aged 6 years).

Location: Church of England 2
Sarah, Lucy & Charles: Line 15, Plot 55, No. 4536.
Peter: Line 15, Plot 55, No. 3383.
Elizabeth, Rose & Mabel: Line 17, Plot 57,
No. 4535.

Cemetery: Mackay Cemetery, Cemetery Road
(bordering Holland, Hume & Shakespeare
Streets), West Mackay, QLD 4740.

In Tropical Queensland cyclones come with the territory. It's part of the cost of living in this idyllic part of the world. Pioneers had the attitude that you just need to get through it and get over it. But over the years some have taken a terrible toll. This is the story of one of them.

Mackay; Saturday 19 January 1918 and the city's 10,000 or so people, who lived at the mouth of the Pioneer River 500 miles or 800 kilometres north of Brisbane, started to realise something was stirring when coastal winds began to pick up. Given 1918 communications technology, there was no way for people to the north to warn Mackay residents a 'big blow' was coming. Not that there were very many people who would have felt the cyclone approaching as it travelled virtually north-east to south-west at a 90-degree angle to the coast.

In 1918 there was no cyclone modelling, where meteorologists predict how a cyclone will track... how fast it will travel or where it will make landfall. There were no radio reports to follow or cyclone warning sirens to alert communities to the danger approaching.

A building threat

The strengthening wind continued throughout the weekend and by Sunday evening was howling, having reached gale force, and reported as *"certainly deserving of the name 'cyclone'".*[1] The good folk of Mackay had only several hours' notice courtesy of a note stuck up on the post office door. They were on their own... at the mercy of what would eventually become a category four cyclone – the second highest category which could pack sustained winds of up to 198 kilometres an hour, gusts to 280, and in this case, a killer storm surge. Of a category four cyclone, the Bureau of Meteorology says:

Significant roofing loss and structural damage. Many caravans destroyed and blown away. Dangerous airborne debris. Widespread power failures.

A Category 4 cyclone's strongest winds are VERY DESTRUCTIVE winds with typical gusts over open flat land of 225 – 279 km/h.

These winds correspond to the highest category on the Beaufort scale, Beaufort 12 (Hurricane).[2]

Wind!

It was wind like most people had never experienced… the wind that causes those in its path to say it 'sounded like a steam train at full tilt… or a jumbo jet taking off.' Wind so strong you can watch it systematically peel layers from buildings until the roof is gone… the walls have vanished and all that is left to resist temporarily is a broken and twisted framework. Not many buildings have a chance as during the passing of a cyclone, the wind can change direction a number of times… attacking from all quarters.

Just before sunrise on Monday morning the unnamed cyclone crossed the coast about 10 kilometres, as the crow flies, north of Mackay, near Dolphin Head. While in all probability it was reasonably calm at the centre of the system, 10 kilometres out the gale would have been howling, leaving the centre of Mackay a sitting duck for the merciless and highly destructive category four winds. And as very often happens in situations where a cyclone is approaching, communications—whatever standard they may be—are first to go.

Flat Top Island lies about six-and-a-half-kilometres off the entrance to the Pioneer River. It was the lighthouse station which would give what news it could of approaching weather, but in this case:

> "*At 11 o' clock (Sunday night) the light keeper at Flat Top reported: Gale had a velocity of 70 miles per hour. That was the last report received from Flat Top, communication having apparently been Interrupted Immediately.*"[3]

Already winds were over 100kph... and strengthening. But soon after daybreak the next morning it was clear what was happening. No outside information was needed to let Mackay residents know they were in a battle to save themselves, their families and whatever they could of their worldly goods and livestock.

The destruction begins

Almost all of the buildings in Mackay were made of timber and none of them was cyclone-proof – building codes and techniques needed to protect them against winds of this strength simply did not exist. Roofs went first, ripped from their rafters with a terrifying screeching sound.

Many of the buildings, built on stumps in the traditional

Queensland way, were lifted by the gales and smashed down on their stumps. Locals reported that when the stumps came up through the front veranda, they put bricks under beds legs and stoves to level things out. Other houses were pitched into the streets with their occupants desperately trying to take shelter inside. And this had been going on throughout the night.

Corrugated iron sheets and smaller lumps of timber became lethal projectiles; in larger sizes they blew from one building to another smashing and crushing. In many cases, your neighbour's house was your worst enemy as it was likely to partially or completely land on yours. Soon most houses in Mackay were damaged to some extent or another; many were uninhabitable.

Sheets of iron torn from rooves in Sydney Street, Mackay, 1918.
Source: State Library of Queensland.

Early estimates were that only two deaths occurred amongst people in wrecked houses... it's a wonder there weren't more. To add to the misery, early in the day it was discovered there was no water or gas available in the mains.

And while destruction reigned it was belting rain. On the day of the cyclone, there was 600mm or nearly 24 inches of rain, the next day 400mm/15.5 inches and the one after that 300mm or nearly 12 inches. It was one of the wettest cyclones in Queensland history. But still the worst was to come – residents were about to realise that it wasn't just the wind tearing their city apart, it was soon to have assistance from a tsunami-like wave which was building.

Water, the enemy

The Harbours and Rivers Engineer's report to parliament said:

> "*The cyclone was accompanied by an elevation in sea surface in the form of a wave which at Mackay slowly rose for about an hour reaching a height of 2.36 metres (8 feet) above the highest spring tide level.*[4]

And on that Monday morning, the impact of that rising sea was about to be felt across the city. Terrible stories started to emerge:

> "*One observer saw a wall of water 7.6m (25 feet) high sweep over the beaches towards the town at 5am 21 January at the height of the cyclone. In 1987 a survivor recalled seeing waves 2.4m (8 feet) to 2.7m (9 feet) high breaking in the centre of Mackay.*"[5]

People were now desperate to escape as the rush of water inundated the lower lying parts of the city. A Miss Morton told how the water arrived at her home at about 4.55am and swamped most of it. It wasn't long before the building collapsed and part of it hit her father, Robert, on the head and he drowned as a result. Miss Morton and her mother drifted separately on rafts of floating debris, managing to keep each other in sight. It was three hours before Miss Morton was rescued… and four hours before her mother was landed.

Georgina Renor, who lived with her grandparents near the viaduct, was found drowned, and it was reported that her grandparents were also missing.

Richard Henry Francis, who was sleeping in a shed at the Show Ground, was killed instantly as the result of the shed collapsing and crushing him.[6]

River Street from the Customs House showing the cyclone damage, 1918.
Source: Kodak Australia, Libraries Australia.

There were terrible stories at every turn. A baby girl died after desperate attempts by her mother to keep her safe; she had carried her youngest child for five hours wrapped in a piece of carpet while they battled to reach a neighbour's house. When she got there, the child had died from exposure.

A family tragedy

At Town Common the Welch family – Peter, his wife Sarah, and children: Elizabeth, 14; Rose, 9; Edwin (Ted), 7; Mabel, 6; Lucy, 3; and Charles aged 3 months—was in dire straits as the weight of wind and water threatened total demolition of their home. Fortunately, two of their children, Emily (Dolly) and Thomas were not in Mackay at the time.

On the Sunday night as the cyclone moved toward Mackay, young Ted Welch asked his mother who would go

Peter and Sarah Welch, 1899. Kindly supplied by the Welch family .

for the milk the next morning. She replied for Ted not to worry about it… it would be too wet. How right she was.

While some accounts suggested Peter attempted to float his family out of danger using part of a wall of the house as a raft, Welch family descendants recall stories of Peter going for help, and are unsure of how the family ended up floating on the wall or how many were on it. Nevertheless, it was a voyage fraught with danger. Elizabeth, the eldest of the children decided to swim for it… to attempt to make it to the Hussey's house nearby. Her body was later found washed up against a shed.

Rose was the next to be lost, apparently swept overboard from the 'raft', and young Ted was definitely rescued from the 'raft' as he floated past the neighbour's house; he was sitting on the floating wall with his legs through the window.[7] Peter also survived but Sarah and her remaining children – Mabel, Lucy and Charles, were lost to the water. Tragically, Sarah's body was located washed up with her hair caught in a fence and baby Charles still in her arms.

Another family's battle

Also battling the cyclone was five-year-old, Eileen Volkman, and her parents, twin sister Edna, and two older sisters. One day in the future, Eileen would marry a surviving Welch son.

Eileen and her family resided in George Street, Mackay, and as the weather worsened, the family fled to a highset house across the paddock which survived and still stands today. Eileen's story is a happier one, with all of her family surviving.

In 1936 Eileen married Thomas Welch who lost his mother, Sarah, and five of his siblings in that devasting cyclone; he

50 George Street. Pictured twins Eileen and Edna Volkman and their mother, Catherine. Below: the wedding portrait of Eileen and Thomas Welch, 1936. Kindly supplied by the Welch family descendants.

was spared by being in Sarina when it struck. At the time of writing this book, Thomas had passed away but Eileen, 105, remembers the cyclone vividly.

"As it came on overnight; you weathered it, and as you found out you had to go, you go. So, we watched and waited until the tank went, and as soon as the tank went at the back of our house, we got out. And that's when the wind blew us over in the paddock."[8]

A terrible toll

Thirty people died in the terrible events of 21 January 1918 in Mackay. It's hard to say, and there appears to be no formal recording of, where or how the majority died. Anecdotally, however, many of the stories centre around bodies in low lying areas or near waterways, suggesting that the tidal wave may have been responsible for most of the fatalities.

Estimates at the time said one thousand buildings in the city were totally destroyed. The brick Town Hall was one of the few things left standing and became home for 60 or so homeless people. Recovery took a long time and it was many months before the lines of tents that accommodated the homeless disappeared from Mackay's showground where they had been set up amongst the fallen trees. The Sydney Street Bridge over the Pioneer River, connecting north and south, collapsed onto a steamer, *The Brinawarr*, which turned turtle... the Captain and his son making a rapid and lucky escape.

Cyclone damage at Pioneer River, 1918. Source: State Library of Queensland.

Mackay was totally cut off from the outside world from early in the cyclonic event. It took five days for the rest of the world to find out what had happened in the coastal sugar town. And it might have been longer were it not for a young man by the name of Jack Vidulich who managed to signal from the roof of the Grand Hotel, using a car headlamp, to the lighthouse keeper on Flat Top Island. Apparently his father had taught the 16-year-old Morse code and he sent the message that told the rest of the world what had happened – how the no-name cyclone had wiped out his town.

So why was it that even though the custom of naming cyclones had been in operation in Queensland for some years, this one had no title? The story goes that the Bureau of Meteorology had only one employee in Mackay and he was on holidays.

The damaged Grand Hotel where Jack Vidulich sent a morse code message about the cyclone damage. Source: State Library of Queensland.

Name or no name, the events of 21 January, and the human toll in Mackay should always be remembered.

How to find the Welch family graves in Mackay Cemetery:

See page 172 for a map to locate the Mackay Cemetery. When you arrive.... drive down Holland Street to find Church of England 2 section... the cemetery will be on your left as you drive down Holland Street. You will see a street sign pointing into the cemetery, take this left into the cemetery and travel straight ahead about 150 metres approximately, past the first intersection. You will find the Welch family graves in between the first and second intersection, and before you get to the break in the trees. The graves are not far from the road. Look for line 15 and line 17: Sarah, Lucy & Charles are in Line 15, Plot 55, No. 4536; Peter is in Line 15, Plot 55, No. 3383; and, Elizabeth, Rose & Mabel are in Line 17, Plot 57; No. 4535.

Cemetery map courtesy of Mackay History.
Visit: http://www.mackayhistory.org/

Acknowledgement:

Our sincere thanks to Cathy Head and the Welch family descendants for their kind assistance with facts and photos.

How to find Mackay Cemetery:

References:

1 THE RUIN OF MACKAY. (1918, January 29). *The Sydney Morning Herald (NSW: 1842 - 1954)*, p. 7. Retrieved July 7, 2018, from http://nla. gov.au/nla.news-article15775337
2 Australian Government. *Bureau of Meteorology*. Tropical Cyclone Intensity and Impacts. http://www.bom.gov.au/cyclone/about/intensity.shtml
3 THE RUIN OF MACKAY. (1918, January 29). Op.cit.
4 Callaghan, Jeff, *Harden Up Queensland*. Case Study Mackay 1918. Dated 9 September 2011. Retrieved 9 July 2018 from URL: http://hardenup.org/ umbraco/customContent/media/631_Mackay_Cyclone_1918.pdf
5 Ibid.
6 THE RUIN OF MACKAY. (1918, January 29). Op.cit.
7 Cathy Head, descendant of the Welch family. From email discussions April to July 2018.
8 After the Storm 1918 Cyclone Interview with Eileen Welch, *Mackay City Council*, Jan 16, 2018. Retrieved 9 July 2018 from URL: https://www. youtube.com/watch?v=yJqJV0a87Qs

Images:

(1918). River St from the Customs House showing cyclone damage, 1918 [picture]. Collection of photographs of the destruction caused by the Mackay cyclone, Qld, Jan 1918. *Kodak, Australia, Libraries Australia*. Retrieved 9 July 2018 from URL: https://trove.nla.gov.au/version/42172196

Unidentified (1918). After a cyclone in Sydney Street, Mackay, 1918. *John Oxley Library, State Library of Queensland*. Retrieved 9 July 2018 from URL: https://trove.nla.gov.au/version/167838821

Unidentified (1918). Cyclone damage at the Pioneer River, Mackay, 1918. *John Oxley Library, State Library of Queensland*. Retrieved 9 July 2018 from URL: https://trove.nla.gov.au/version/47937727

Unidentified (1918). Cyclone damage to the Grand Hotel, Mackay, 1918. *John Oxley Library, State Library of Queensland*. Retrieved 9 July 2018 from URL: https://trove.nla.gov.au/version/167838891

1936 Eileen (nee Volkman) and Tom Welch wedding photo. Kindly supplied by Cathy Head and the Welch family descendants, 2018.

The Volkman family home at 50 George Street with Eileen, twin Edna and mother Catherine present, and the 1899 Peter and Sarah Welch photo, kindly supplied by Cathy Head and the Welch family descendants, 2018.

Mackay Cemetery Map courtesy of Mackay History: www.mackayhistory.org

Maps: ©OpenStreetMap contributors. www.openstreetmap.org/copyright

The 19 orphans of Mackay

Interred:[1]

William Baker, 1879 - 10 Aug 1885 (aged 6 years);
Henry Bergan, 1875 - 13 June 1884 (aged 9 years);
Eva Mary Boland, 1883 - 29 March 1885 (aged 2 years);
Loftus Buckley, 1880 - 2 Oct 1885 (aged 5 years);
Michael Francis Callaghan, 1877 - 3 March 1882 (aged 5 years);
Richard Beagley, 17 February – 17 Oct 1883 (aged 10 months);
Patrick Hall, 1876 - 2 August 1880 (aged 4 years);
Mary Kate Halligan, 1878 - 19 July 1884 (aged 6 years);
Patrick Halligan, 1873 - 8 June 1884 (aged 11 years);
Henry Vincent Long, 1877 - 16 Nov 1885 (aged 8 years);
Margaret Lynch, 1879 - 2 July 1883 (aged 4 years);
Ernest May, 1882 - 27 January 1885 (aged 3 years);
Joseph Richardson, 1879 - 8 July 1883 (aged 4 years);
Henry Roll, 6 February 1876 -1885 (aged 9 years);
Walter Rolls, 1879 - 2 June 1885 (aged 6 years);
Thomas William Simmonds, 1882 - 20 Jan 1885 (aged 3 years);
Joseph Charles Smyth, 1875 - 7 Dec 1884 (aged 9 years);
Alice Armstrong Strong, 1870 - 25 Mar 1882 (aged 12 years);
Charles Turner, 1879 - 26 April 1881 (aged 2 years).

Location:	Undetermined. At the time of writing this book, local author, Doug Petersen, continues to investigate possible site locations for the original burial ground.[2]
Cemetery:	No known markers exist for the burial site.
Interred:	Father Pierre-Marie Bucas
Location:	Catholic Section 2, Row 1, Plot 60-66
Cemetery:	Mackay Cemetery, Cemetery Rd, West Mackay, QLD 4740.

Four-year-old Patrick Hall's dad agreed to pay five shillings a week to the orphanage to look after his son, but he never paid. Henry Bergen, nine, wasn't well when he arrived at St Joseph's Orphanage with his sister, Ellen; Ernest May, three, was taken from his mother who was living with a Chinaman who wasn't his father. Four-year-old Margaret Lynch was destitute and illegitimate – her mother Anne was a servant, a Catholic girl who must have fallen on hard times… Margaret's father was listed as unknown, and Margaret had been removed from the Benevolent Asylum Rockhampton and sent to St Joseph's.[3] During the 11 years from 1874 – 1885, the Mackay orphanage was home to around 40 to 90 children,[4] with 126 children over time listed in the admissions' book.[5]

Children came, went, died and survived, after starting their lives as wards of the church. St Joseph's Orphanage was a home for the abandoned, uncontrollable, illegitimate (children of single parents, mixed race, and other misguided terms), children taken forcibly from their Aboriginal mothers, children abandoned by a widowed or remarried parent, children from poverty, and children of the 'insane' housed in lunatic asylums as they were then called… it was a very different time.[6]

Renowned Mackay resident, Eileen Welch, 105, whose family feature in the Mackay Cyclone story in this book learned that her "father Edmond Volkman and brothers Frederick and Paul were placed in the orphanage in 1883 following the death of their father and the admission of their mother to the Woogaroo Lunatic Asylum near Brisbane."[7] When their mother had recovered five months later, the boys were returned to her care. Incidents like this were not uncommon. But our story is about 19 young orphans who would never leave St Joseph's Orphanage.

How the orphanage began

It was built with the best intentions… Catholic Priest, Father Pierre Bucas—who would become a much loved and respected resident—founded the orphanage and left its running to the Sisters of St Joseph for the first three years and later to the Sisters of Mercy.[8]

A well-travelled man, Father Bucas was born in Brittany, France, studied for the priesthood in Rome, was ordained in New Zealand and then spent 36 years as a parish priest in Mackay.[9] Somewhat incongruent to the faith (one might think), Father Bucas answered the call when Pope Pius IX appealed to Catholic France for volunteers to assist in defending the Papal States in the Italian Wars of unification. It was not unusual at the time for priests to be soldiers; the Pope maintained a fighting army up until the late 1800s.[10] Father Bucas served as a Corporal until he took a bullet above the knee and was relieved of his duty.[11] It was through volunteering to assist Bishop Pompallier in New Zealand that the good Father found his way to our shores, but not without incident. The three-month journey by sea proved eventful with friction between the ship's captain and crew, resulting in the crew being placed in irons. It was the earnest pleading of Father Bucas that assisted with their liberation after a trial in Auckland.[12]

Father Bucas arrived in 1869 in Mackay – the very year it was proclaimed a municipality. *The Catholic Press* wrote

Father Bucas (standing) with Bishop James Duhig of Rockhampton (1905-1912), at Mackay. Source: John Oxley Library, State Library of Queensland.

that when the "Sisters of Mercy were sent to Mackay, the first church, built there by Father Bucas, became the convent school, and continued so until it was blown away in the 1918 cyclone."[13] It was an eventful life!

On the outskirts of Mackay, Father Bucas secured 2880 acres[14] and this became the location of St Joseph's Orphanage. The Government offered to conduct the orphanage as a state institution, but Father Bucas declined the offer, and later an endowment from the Premier, Sir Thomas McIlwraith, provided nine pence per child per week and a salary to the Sisters similar to State school teachers. Father Bucas remained in charge and it remained a Catholic institution.[15] His intentions were good; poverty was prevalent in the town and its outreaches and the sufferers touched his heart.[16]

Life in the orphanage

The orphanage buildings were "situated on a low sandy ridge separated from the sea in front by a strip of forest and closely surrounded on all other three sides by a large [mangrove] swamp. The orphanage consisted of a house for the priest to live in when he visited, a two-storey dwelling for the nuns and a dormitory on the ground level for the children."[17]

And this 'swamp' would prove problematic for our young charges, especially Patrick, Henry, Ernest and Margaret. The children began to get sick, and the death count began to rise.

The admission certificates for the children list a variety of malaise from consumption to disease of the heart. Given the orphanage was built in proximity to a swamp, it was a perfect breeding ground for mosquitos – of which the female species can be carriers of malaria. But initially, the smell of the swamp—its airborne odour—was thought to be responsible for the spate of ill-health.[18] After all, the orphans slept about two feet (600mm) from the ground on the lower floor of the building, and the nuns slept on the upper level. But only the children were in poor health.[19]

Dr Arthur Cutfield, the Heath and Government Medical Officer in Mackay visited the orphanage and in 1884 he wrote in correspondence:

"A large number of children have an extremely unhealthy appearance, and several suffer or have suffered from

Ernest May

Where born: Townsville

When born: 1881

When admitted: 10 . 3 . 84

Why admitted: To rescue the child from the hands of Chinamen with whom the mother is living, the child being the offspring of a white man would very likely be ill treated.

On what terms admitted:

When discharged:

To whom discharged:

For what purpose discharged:

Name of Parents: Illegitimate

Ernest May and Patrick Hall's extracts from the admission register to St Joseph's Orphanage. Source: Queensland State Archives.

4

Freddy or Patrick Mannann or Hall

Where born: Supposed to be at Bundaberg

When born: 1877

When admitted: 1 May 1880   Religion R.C.

Why admitted:

On what terms admitted: Father agreed to pay 5/ weekly but failed to do so

When discharged: Died of consumption of the glands 1. 8. 1880

To whom discharged:

an affection of the heart produced by debility; I believe them to be suffering from malarial disease produced by the situation of the orphanage, which lies between a swamp and the sea – the swamp, in which there is always stagnant water, being almost immediately behind the buildings."[20]

In 1885 in a report he continued to voice his concerns, saying:

"(They) are... closely surrounded on all the other three sides by a large swamp, the surface of which is only a few feet lower than the ground on which the Orphanage buildings stand. It is easy to see, then, that if this swamp be malarious the inhabitants of the Orphanage must be exposed to the malarial poisoning in an intense form... it is a well-known fact that the malarious poisoning is most dangerous at night and that it does not extend far from the ground in a vertical direction; now, the sleeping apartment of the sisters is the only portion of the buildings not situated on the ground, being placed at a considerable height over the children's dining place and this, I think, would go far to explain their immunity."[21]

Dr Cutfield monitored the children's health and noted:

"At my last visit four children were seriously ill and they were all in this extremely anaemic condition. I found fourteen others showing the same symptoms. It gives a proportion of one in every three who is in very delicate health."[22]

Dr Cani [Bishop of the diocese of Rockhampton][23] responded:

"For years past the said buildings have been in the present locality, which has not been considered objectionable except by Dr Cutfield... Probably the long drought may be the cause of the unhealthy appearance of the children."[24]

Relocating the orphanage

Dr Cutfield outlined his concerns. Worried that the children were at risk, government officials suggested the orphanage be closed and the children transferred to St Vincent's Orphanage at Nudgee, near Brisbane.[25] Dr Cani had another idea and recommended a suitable site be found in Rockhampton (in his jurisdiction).[26]

Government authorities gave permission and then the people of Mackay protested, considering the orphanage their own, despite the decision having already been made. Dr Cutfield then went on to say in support of the current establishment and staff, that: "These good sisters fought against sickness, malaria, and all the ills caused by the unhealthy position of the Orphanage. Yet they kept it clean and sweet, they did their best for the children in face of every difficulty and discouragement."[27]

In 1885 the orphanage was relocated and a new orphanage known as Meteor Park was built 11 kilometres from Rockhampton. Father Bucas was not involved in the running of Meteor Park. The 57 remaining children (or 75 in some reports) at St Joseph's orphanage in Mackay arrived on 22 December 1885. This orphanage was later known as 'Neerkol'.[28] The newspaper reported on the children: "They constituted a heavy charge, for all were sickly and for some time their condition necessitated almost daily visits by Dr McNeely."[29]

An image of Neerkol orphanage circa 1910 – 1930.
Source: Find and Connect, Commonwealth of Australia.

Despite all his efforts, perhaps Father Bucas did not feel he had the support of the community regarding the orphanage. A letter from him tabled during the relocation discussion stated: "I must re-assert that the Orphanage was not 'got up', neither was it supported by the people."[30] "He agreed with Sister Hardiman, who had been in charge of the orphanage, that 'little had been done for the orphanage by the people of Mackay. He stated that he had paid the rents on the land out of his own means, and that he had provided every article in connection with the orphanage except for eight head of cattle'.... The press commented that Father Bucas' remarks would not find favour with the people of Mackay."[31]

After the relocation, the reality of the situation was captured in *The Mackay Mercury and South Kennedy Advertiser*, two days before Christmas 1885:

> *"The children, who had been removed from St Joseph's Orphanage, left for Rockhampton, and the scene of this unpleasant business is over. A few of the children, who have gone South, are doomed to die within the next few years, but it is to be hoped that change of air will restore many of them to health."*[32]

Ten of the children did in fact die within months of arrival.[33] It was not until some years later that the cause of the children's decline in health was identified as hookworm[34] – a parasite that latches onto the wall of the small intestine and feeds on blood. In children, it stunted development, made them weak and tired.[35] At St Joseph's 23 orphans fell ill. Of these 19 died and were buried at Bucasia, four died after admission to Mackay Hospital and were buried in Mackay Cemetery; a significant number if you consider this is a third of the orphanage's inhabitants. [36]

Finding their resting place

There's been much speculation as to where the 19 children rest. There are no gravestones or memorial to mark their graves. No doubt funds were short, and headstones were an unnecessary expense for these young abandoned ones.

But it is interesting to note that if the children weren't baptised on arrival at the orphanage or if of no religious persuasion, they were baptised Catholic, and even more interesting that the deceased children were not believed to have been buried in consecrated ground.[37] It is believed that the former site of St Joseph's orphanage is identifiable by the mature fruit trees that were planted by the orphanage inhabitants.[38] It is possible that the children rest in this area.

What became of…

The children mentioned at the start of this story, were four of the 19 children who did not survive St Joseph's Orphanage:

Patrick Hall, four, died of consumption of the glands. He was admitted to the orphanage on 11 May 1880 and died less than eleven weeks later, on 1 August.

Henry Bergen, nine, was born on 25 April 1875 and was not placed in St Joseph's orphanage until 24 June 1883, when he was aged 8. His sister, Ellen, was also admitted with him. Henry arrived with consumption and his admission form reads: "He was in consumption when he came to the orphanage but lingered on for a whole year." [39] He died two weeks short of a year to the day of his admission, on 13 June 1884.

Margaret Lynch, four, was admitted as a destitute and illegitimate little girl on 14 November 1881. She died fromdisease of the heart on the 2 July 1883, less than two years after her admission.

Ernest May, three, who was thought to be at risk because of his situation living with "Chinamen" as his admission form stated: as "offspring of a white man would very likely be ill-treated"[40] died in the orphanage 10 months after he was admitted, cause unknown.

In poor health, **Father Pierre Bucas** left Mackay in 1913 to 'retire' to Barcaldine with his nephew, Fr. Julien Plormel.[41] He died in Rockhampton on 26 October 1930, aged 90. He was initially buried in Rockhampton but was later returned to the old Mackay Cemetery, where you can visit his grave. You will also find a memorial to Father Bucas on the Bucasia Esplanade.[42] At his requiem mass, it was said: "His name will live in the Australian Catholic Church history as that of the grand old pioneer priest of Northern and Central Queensland."[43]

A greater tribute was paid in the local paper, when Father Bucas left Mackay in 1880 for Port Douglas/Cairns:

"What is remarkable is the fact that a number of the prominent members of the various Protestant churches assembled, with the Mayor presiding... crowds of all denominations assembled to bid him farewell... As the little vessel steamed away from the wharf, those present realised painfully that they had parted from a friend whose loss will not be easily supplied."[44]

In 1938 the town of Seaview was renamed Bucasia after Father Bucas.

Remembering them

Today there is nothing to mark the St Joseph's Orphanage site in Mackay, and no graves to visit. But west of Rockhampton, there is the beautiful Children's Memorial Garden Neerkol on Meteor Park Road. Featuring gardens, statues and tiny footprints on the cement path leading through the garden.

Also, a former resident of the Neerkol Orphanage,

The beautiful Children's Memorial Garden Neerkol.
Source: Central Queensland Family History Association.

Hannelore Worrall, organised the construction of a memorial using bricks and a metal sign from the original gates. The memorial gates are several hundred metres away from the original gates that lead to the Neerkol Orphanage, on the Capricorn Highway and Power Station Road, Kabra. They pay tribute to both the local children and British orphans who passed through that institution.

An inscription reads:

"Over 4000 children passed through these gates between 11 April 1885 when the first 11 children arrived, to its closure on 5 March 1978. It is our wish that in creating this Neerkol Memorial not one baby, little child, young adult or Neerkol worker will ever be forgotten."[45]

And, we remember the 19 orphaned children who never left St Joseph's Orphanage. The swamp in the west of the Bucasia locality is, still to this day, known as Orphanage Swamp. [46]

We respectfully acknowledge the suffering of many children during their time in orphanages in Queensland and Australia-wide; not only from the duress of being without the security of a family, but the physical, sexual and psychological abuse suffered by some of the children that has since come to light through the inquiry into the abuse of children in Queensland institutions. To date, compensation claims were settled on behalf of more than 70 former Neerkol residents.[47]

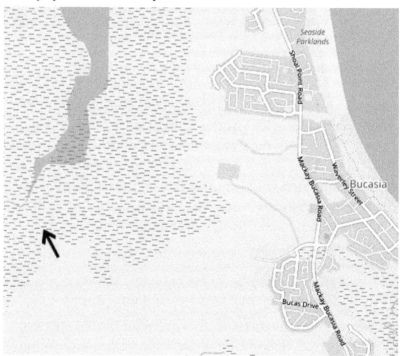

Map with approximate orphanage location based on: Orphanage Swamp – Wetland, Ref no. 25585, Local Govt, Mackay Regional. Design: Open Map.

How to find Father Bucas' grave in Catholic Section 2, Row 1, Plot 60-66:

To locate West Mackay Cemetery, refer to the map on page 172. To find Father Bucas' grave, drive down Cemetery Road, heading towards Hume Street and you will find Catholic Section 2 in that triangular corner, before the drain and next to Catholic Section 1. Turn into the last path on your right before you come to Hume Street. Father Bucas' grave is in the first row.

Acknowledgement:

Our sincere thanks to Doug Petersen, author of *St Joseph's Orphanage Merara*; Sister Joanne Molloy, Sisters of Mercy Archivist; Glenn Hall, *Mackay History*; and Neridah Kaddatz, biographer, for their assistance in the research of this story.

Father Bacus' grave and location. Photos: courtesy of Neridah Kaddatz.

References:

1 Hall, Glen, St Joseph's Orphanage Cemetery (Bucasia), *Mackay History*, 18 July 2107. Retrieved 4 July 2018 from URL: http://www.mackayhistory.org/research/cemeteries/orphanage.html

2 Petersen, Doug, *St Joseph's Orphanage Merara*, Rural View, Queensland. Published November 2017. Refer: https://trove.nla.gov.au/version/253794013

3 Queensland State Archives Item ID313137, Register - admissions to St Joseph's Orphanage, Mackay, *The Queensland Government*, 11/5/1880 - 4/8/1884. Retrieved 5 July 2018 from URL: http://www.archivessearch.qld.gov.au/Search/ItemDetails.aspx?ItemId=313137

4 QUEENSLAND GRAND OLD PIONEER. (30 October 1930). *The Catholic Press* (Sydney, NSW: 1895 - 1942), p. 19. Retrieved July 4, 2018, from http://nla.gov.au/nla.news-article106251295

5 Petersen, Doug, in conversation by email 30/7/18. Op.cit.

6 - 7 Meixner, Sophie, and Philpott, Tegan, Final resting place of 19 children who died in a Mackay orphanage in late 1800s a local mystery, *ABC Tropical North*, 30 Nov 2017. Retrieved 5 July 2018 from URL: http://www.abc.net.au/news/2017-11-30/final-resting-place-of-19-children-who-died-in-mackay-orphanage/9205194

8 Hall, Glen. Op.cit.

9 A Heritage Walk, Mackay cemetery, 5th edition, 2010, *Mackay Regional Council*. Retrieved 4 July 2018 from URL: http://www.mackay.qld.gov.au/__data/assets/pdf_file/0005/89492/Cemetery_Walk.pdf

10 Kaddatz, Neridah, author of a pending biography on Father Bacus. Email discussion, 26 July 2018.

11 - 13 QUEENSLAND GRAND OLD PIONEER. (1930, October 30). *The Catholic Press* (Sydney, NSW: 1895 - 1942), p. 19. Retrieved July 4, 2018, from http://nla.gov.au/nla.news-article106251295

14 Wright, Berenice, A Change is as Good as…" Changing Frontiers, Chapter 12 in Pearn, John, & Cobcroft, Mervyn, Ed., Fevers & Frontiers, Amphion Press, 1990.

15 QUEENSLAND GRAND OLD PIONEER. Op.cit.

16 Wright, Berenice, (2009). Op.cit.

17 Hall, Glen. Op.cit.

18 Meixner, Sophie, and Philpott, Tegan, Op.cit.

19 - 20 Wright, Berenice & Clarke, Lara (2009). Op.cit.

21 Roderick, Donald Charles, *The origins of the elevated Queensland house*, Bachelor of Architecture (UQ) - A thesis, School of Geography, Planning & Architecture. Retrieved 4 July 2018 from URL: https://bit.ly/2MRPmID

22 Meixner, Sophie, and Philpott, Tegan. Op.cit.

23 QUEENSLAND GRAND OLD PIONEER. Op.cit.

24 - 26 Wright, Berenice. Op.cit.

27 No title (22 Aug 1885). *Mackay Mercury and South Kennedy Advertiser* (Qld: 1867-1887), p2. Retrieved 4 July 2018 from http://nla.gov.au/nla.news-article169699336

28 Hall, Glen. Op.cit.

29 Fifty Years of Noble Work (16 May 1935). *The Central Queensland Herald*, p 60. Retrieved 6 July 2018 from http://nla.gov.au/nla.news-article7036038

30 No title (22 Aug 1885). *Mackay Mercury and South Kennedy Advertiser*. Op.cit.

31 Wright, Berenice. Op.cit.
32 Local and other News. (1885, December 23). *Mackay Mercury and South Kennedy Advertiser (Qld.: 1867 - 1887)*, p. 2. Retrieved July 5, 2018, from http://nla.gov.au/nla.news-article169699250
33 Petersen, Doug, in conversation by email 30/7/18. Op.cit.
34 DEATH AT NINETY (1930, October 24). *Morning Bulletin (Rockhampton, Qld: 1878-1954)*, p14. Retrieved 5 July 2018, from http://nla.gov.au/nla.news-article54678042
35 Delgado, Amanda/reviewed by Murrell, D., MD Hookworm Infections, *Healthline*, 2018. Retrieved 5 July 2018 from: https://www.healthline.com/health/hookworm#causes
36 Petersen, Doug, in conversation by email 30/7/18. Op.cit.
37 Meixner, Sophie, and Philpott, Tegan. Op.cit.
38 Hall, Glen. Op.cit.
39-40 Queensland State Archives Item ID313137. Op.cit.
41 Kaddatz, Neridah, email discussion July 2018. Op.cit.
42 Hall, Glen. Op.cit.
43 - 44 QUEENSLAND GRAND OLD PIONEER. Op.cit.
45 - 46 (2003-08-05). *Neerkol Orphans Memorial* summary, published 5 August 2003. Retrieved 5 July 2015 from URL: https://trove.nla.gov.au/version/165430502
47 "Orphanage Swamp (entry 25585)". Queensland Place Names. Queensland Government. Retrieved 13 July 2018 from URL: https://bit.ly/2JjdXUg

Images:

Despite all efforts, we were unable to find any images of St Joseph's Orphanage. The orphanage photo at the start of this story is Nudgee Orphanage, once considered as a transfer venue for the children.

Unidentified. (2008). *Children at Nudgee Orphanage, Ca. 1928*, Collection reference: API-81 Dept of Public Instruction-Dental Service Photograph Album. *John Oxley Library, State Library of Queensland.* Retrieved 6 July 2018 from URL: http://hdl.handle.net/10462/deriv/7378

- Father Bucas' grave photos courtesy of Neridah Kaddatz.

-Unidentified Bishop James Duhig of Rockhampton, at Mackay, with Father Bucas. *John Oxley Library, State Library of Queensland.* Retrieved 4 July 2018 from URL: https://trove.nla.gov.au/version/167825635

-Admission records: *Queensland State Archives* Item ID313137, Register-admissions to St Joseph's Orphanage, Mackay, The Qld Government, 11/5/1880 - 4/8/1884. Retrieved 5 July 2018 from: http://www.archivessearch.qld.gov.au/Search/ItemDetails.aspx?ItemId=313137

- [Photographer unknown], St Joseph's Home, Neerkol c1910-1930, *Find and Connect,* Commonwealth of Australia. 2011 , Retrieved 6 July 2018 from URL: https://www.findandconnect.gov.au/ref/qld/objects/QD0000281.htm

- The Children's Memorial Garden Neerkol, Central Queensland Family History Association. Retrieved 15 July 2018 from: https://sites.google.com/site/qfamilyhistory/articles-indexes/history/orphanages/st-joseph-s-home-neerkol

- Orphanage Swamp – Wetland, Ref no. 25585, *Local Government, Mackay Regional,* 1 January 1970. Retrieved 6 July 2018 from URL: https://bit.ly/2JjdXUg

- Maps: ©OpenStreetMap contributors. www.openstreetmap.org/copyright

In Memoriam
of

WILLIAM CLARENCE
ELDEST SON OF
THANKFUL & ELIZA WILLMETT
BORN JULY 29ᵀᴴ 1858
DIED JUNE 15ᵀᴴ 1884
AGED 25 YEARS
AND OF

ELSPETH MAY
YOUNGEST DAUGHTER OF THE ABOVE
BORN MAY 9ᵀᴴ 1870
DIED NOV. 19ᵀᴴ 1871
AGED 18 MONTHS
ALSO

ELIZA ANNE
BELOVED WIFE OF T. WILLMETT
DIED 1ˢᵀ MAY 1899
AGED 63 YEARS.
ALSO

WALTER HENRY
BELOVED SON OF
THANKFUL AND ELIZA ANNE WILLMETT
DIED 4ᵀᴴ SEPTEMBER 1905
AGED 30 YEARS.
ALSO THE ABOVE

THANKFUL WILLMETT.
DIED 2ᴺᴰ AUGUST 1907,
AGED 76 YEARS.

Thankful Willmett's grave. Photo: Abraham Pitman.

Splitting the difference
Thankful Percy Willmett

Interred: Thankful Percy Willmett, 1831 – 21 August 1907 (aged 76 years).

Location: Block A, Row 1, Grave 2.

Cemetery: West End Cemetery, 33 Church Street, Townsville, QLD 4810.

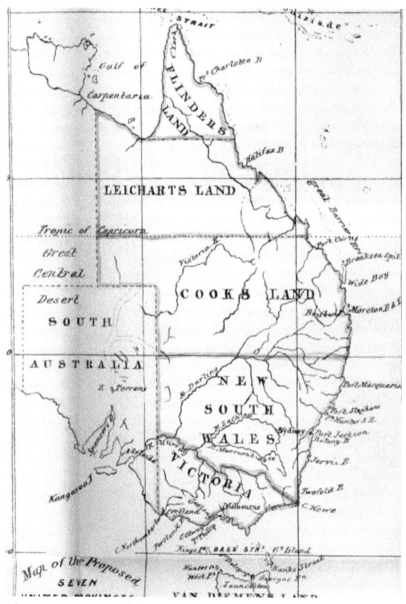

The J.D. Lang Map of the proposed divisions, 1857. Lang proposes three divisions for Queensland. Source: Fryer Library, University of Queensland.

Any way you want to look at it, it's an extremely large place. *Queensland!*

It's nearly five times the size of Japan, seven times the size of Great Britain, and two and a half times the size of Texas.[1]

It probably got this big because the early architects of statehood in Australia... like just about everyone else at the time the continent was being divided up... assumed it would get split at least a couple more times before the final boundaries were settled – it just made sense... but that often counts for little.

John Dunmore Lang—the man who had Lang Park, the place where Queensland/NSW State of Origin footy started, named after him—had been influential in the separation of Victoria and Queensland from NSW.

He believed there should be at least seven states along Australia's eastern seaboard, three of them occupying where Queensland is now. By 1857 he already had them named – Flinders Land in the north, Leichardts Land in the centre and Cooks Land in the south. Note that he also had some of the best parts of the NSW-owned Northern Rivers in Cooks Land.[2]

And anyway, many thought Queensland had its capital in the wrong place so there would have to be at least one more northern headquarters. Yes... it all made sense but despite much hullabaloo that's lasted more than a century and a half, the fine print just made it all too hard.

A city too far south

It was the placement of the capital city, Brisbane, that drove much of the early impetus for a new northern state, with some likening putting the capital so far south to placing the heart in the big toe to help circulation in the body. As someone pointed out – do you think there would be equal treatment of people who lived at Croydon, one thousand miles (1600km) from Brisbane and those from Ipswich, just 20 miles (32km) away?

So, where should a capital city be and what should be the factors that decided that? Some have suggested it was the shape of the state that had already begun to throw up candidates for capital cities simply by the way a particular area operated. It was no coincidence that all the early railways in Queensland ran east-west in isolation, linking the bush with coastal ports. Cairns, Townsville, Bowen, Mackay and Rockhampton at one end... Mareeba, Hughenden, Guthalungra, Eton and Mirani, and Longreach at the other. The northern coastal railway link-up wasn't completed until 1924.

Those who wanted a new state in the north had seen what had happened as other state capital cities began to dominate colonial parliaments, leaving those furthest from the corridors of power feeling under-represented and ignored. So, those wanting divisions—the separatists—believed there were plenty of reasons for there to be at least one new state north of Brisbane on the grounds of the location of the capital and equal treatment of all, especially when it came to the allocation of funds for public works.

The separationists at work

These were the central themes of most of the separation movements that began as early as 1866 when Queensland itself was in its infancy. There were many individual separatist movements arising from numbers of different settlements after the first in Bowen. But it wasn't until the 1880s that the most concerted and organised effort at separation took place. It centred on Townsville and was headed by a man with the unusual name of Thankful Percy Willmett.

Thankful Willmett was born in London and became a ship's officer, sailing on the transports that took troops to the Crimean War and later on an emigrant ship on the run to Australia. He eventually resigned and became an immigrant himself, settling initially in Central Queensland around 1858. There, amongst other things, he ran the Clarendon Hotel in Rockhampton and later the Commercial in Nebo.[3]

When the Cape York gold rushes began he, like thousands of others, was drawn to the Palmer River field where he made enough money running a shop and acting as the post-

Thankful Willmett, 1887. Source: City Libraries, Townsville.

master to set up a printing business in Townsville. He rapidly became active in civic life and by 1880 was the Mayor of the burgeoning metropolis.

But having observed the development of Central and Northern Queensland for close to two decades, Thankful became caught up in the fight for a new state in the north. He threw himself into the effort and before long was the president of the North Queensland Separation Council, devoting with enthusiasm his ability in the struggle to free the north of the fetters linking it with the south.[4] And he didn't mince his words. He maintained that Northerners had:

> "Left to them not the slightest real control over their own political affairs, their public loans, or other public works... And, whether they petition or protest, they are met with the reply that Queensland is under responsible Government."[5]

THE SEPARATION QUESTION.

[BY ELECTRIC TELEGRAPH.]

[FROM OUR OWN CORRESPONDENT.]

Townsville, Sunday, April 12.

The Separation Convention met again yesterday morning, at 10 o'clock; twenty delegates were present. A council was formed, consisting of the president (Mr. Willmett), the vice-presidents (Messrs. Aheroe and Tucker), the treasurer (Mr. Hays), and Messrs. Taylor, Goldring, and M'Intosh, with two delegates from each branch of the Separation League, to conduct the business of the movement. Townsville is to be the head-quarters of the council, but members from branch leagues will be allowed to vote by wire. Provision was made for the necessary funds. It was resolved that the council should use its influence to procure the return of separationists to the Brisbane Parliament in the event of their election in the North.

Source: Qld Times 16 April 1885, Ipswich Herald & General Advertiser.

Taking up the fight

The movement, under his leadership, petitioned the British to intervene, which would have been possible before federation. The Melbourne *Argus* reported on 23 June 1886:

"The signatures to the petition which will be despatched to London before the end of this month have exceeded expectation, numbering now 10,200. The whole body of electors on the last northern roll having amounted to some 12,000 only, there can be little question on the score of unanimity."[6]

But almost 12 months after that newspaper story, Thankful and the Separation Council received a major setback. The petition to London had not persuaded the Secretary of State for the Colonies that he and his government needed to do anything. His view was, apparently, that Queensland was self-governing and he would not intervene unless requested to do so by that Parliament.

As Thankful put it in a letter to the *Brisbane Courier*: *"Our case is not considered sufficiently strong to justify Government exercising latent power without resolution by the Queensland Parliament."*[7] He knew what chance there was of the Queensland Parliament calling in the British government. Thankful was bitterly disappointed but not defeated:

"Unless we have miserably degenerated from the independent, manly pioneers who brought commerce to our coast, and started cattle over our Western Downs, we shall not accept tamely and cringingly this rejection of our claim to live under a constitutional Government capable of developing our resources and rewarding our exertions... We need not cherish angry resentment while we stand firm to our purpose, that soon or later we will obtain a release from Southern supremacy, and that North Queensland shall take her place, independent and self-governed, among the colonies of Australia."[8]

By the early 1890s, the succession movement in North Queensland had all but fizzled out. In his time at the helm of the North Queensland Separation Council, Thankful Willmett had been considered the 'father' of the separation movement seeking independence from Brisbane but the complicated manner by which it could only be achieved defeated him and everyone else who tried before and after.

Perhaps by the 1890s there were other issues competing for attention... like the national industrial situation, dominated by the Maritime Dispute and the ongoing Shearers' strike, the closure of banks and the economic depression which affected rich and poor.

Thankful Percy Willmett died on 21 August 1907 at the age of 76. He and his wife, Eliza, had five children, two boys and three girls. He had been mayor of Townsville four times, established a thriving business—T. Willmett & Sons Printing *(pictured)*—which was run by members of his family until 1980, and had been the leader of the move for a new state in the north through its most promising phase. Willmett Street in Townsville city is named for him.

Willmett's stationery warehouse in Flinders Street, Townsville in 1913. It was constructed in 1883 and remained in the family until 1980. Source: City Libraries, Townsville.

Don't say one day

No doubt there are those who still believe that one day it will happen... that John Dunmore Lang's vision of multiple states where Queensland now lies will come to pass, or that maybe there will simply be a division of what we know as Queensland.

In March 2018 Robbie Katter, from the Katter Australia Party called for a costing on splitting the state north and south. He has suggested a new boundary dividing the two along the Tropic of Capricorn, putting Rockhampton in the north... but the rapidly developing and wealthy mining centre of Emerald in the south.

Good Luck Robbie!

Maybe we need to call in the sporting administrators... they've had northern and southern teams competing well on the national rugby league stage for years. Perhaps they can sort it out... and it would give State of Origin a whole new meaning... but then again, who gets to be the maroons?

How to find Thankful Willmett's grave in West End Cemetery:

Thankful's headstone also carries the names of several other members of the family and his is right at the bottom.

Enter the cemetery from Church Street by the gate that is adjacent to the park, almost opposite where Mary Street joins Church Street. The Willmett grave is in the second row on your left immediately beside the unmade internal road. If you refer to the photo on page 192, you will see its location in proximity to the fenceline.

How to find West End Cemetery, Church Street, Townsville:

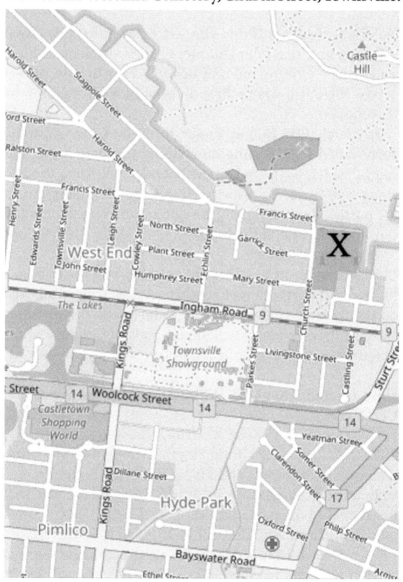

Maps: ©OpenStreetMap contributors. www.openstreetmap.org/copyright

References:

1 Interesting facts about Queensland, *Queensland Government*, 7 December, 2017. Retrieved 17 July 2018 from URL: https://www.qld.gov.au/about/about-queensland/statistics-facts/facts

2 Lang, J.D., Map of the proposed seven united provinces of eastern Australia, 1857. Collection of the Fryer Library, *University of Queensland* 12 November 2010. Retrieved 17 July 2018 from URL: http://www.qhatlas.com.au/map/jdlang-map-proposed-seven-united-provinces-eastern-australia-1857

3 *The Willmett Family Notes*. Retrieved July 14, 2018 from URL: http://www3.sympatico.ca/rupertlt/willmettf/pafn02.htm

4 DEATH OF MR. T. WILLMETT. (1907, August 22). *Townsville Daily Bulletin (Qld.: 1907 - 1954)*, p. 4. Retrieved July 14, 2018, from http://nla.gov.au/nla.news-article57769158

5 Doran, C.R., Separation Movements in North Queensland In the Nineteenth Century. *University of Queensland*, 1978.

6 The Northern Queensland Separation Movement. (1886, June 23). *The Argus (Melbourne, Vic.: 1848 - 1957)*, p. 10. Retrieved July 14, 2018, from http://nla.gov.au/nla.news-article6099689

7 & 8 North Queensland Separation Council. (1887, June 25). *The Brisbane Courier (Qld.: 1864 - 1933)*, p. 6. Retrieved July 14, 2018, from http://nla.gov.au/nla.news-article3472810

Images:

Lang, J.D., Map of the proposed seven united provinces of eastern Australia, 1857, (2nd edition) Sydney, Cunninghame, 1857. *Fryer Library, University of Queensland*, 12 November 2010. Retrieved 17 July 2018 from URL: http://www.qhatlas.com.au/map/jdlang-map-proposed-seven-united-provinces-eastern-australia-1857

Mr. Thankful Percy Willmett, of the Townsville Council, 1887 [picture]. Kindly supplied by *City Libraries, Townsville*. Retrieved 17 July 2018 from URL: https://townsville.spydus.com/cgi-bin/spydus.exe/ENQ/PIC/BIBENQ?IRN=12427064&FMT=PA

(1885, April 16). *Queensland Times, Ipswich Herald & General Advertiser (Qld.: 1861-1908)*, p4. Retrieved 17 July 2018 from: http://nla.gov.au/nla.news-page9662333

Willmett's stationery warehouse, Flinders Street, 1913. [picture] Kindly supplied by *City Libraries, Townsville*. Retrieved 17 July 2018 from URL:https://townsville.spydus.com/cgi-bin/spydus.exe/ENQ/PIC/BIBENQ?IRN=12419952&FMT=PA

Thankful Willmett grave photo by Abraham Pitman, Townsville.

Maps: ©OpenStreetMap contributors. www.openstreetmap.org/copyright

Charles 'Jack' John Miles' grave. Photo: Abraham Pitman.

A boy's own adventure
Charles 'Jack' John Miles

Interred: Charles 'Jack' John Miles, 1913 – 7 September 1943 (aged 30 years).

Location: Section C, Grave No. 8, Row A.

Cemetery: Townsville War Cemetery, 62 Evans Street, Belgian Gardens, QLD 4810.

*Taken on the wing of Catalina A24-49 on 6 May 1943. Rear row, L to R: Dawson Wilson, Bernie McInerney, Ron Smith, Fred Darby, Reg Weeks. Front row, L to R: Max Dore, Gordon Hockey, **Jack Miles** (pilot), Bert Fowler. Source: from Ms Eileen Ponsford (Jack's sister, deceased) and reprinted with thanks to Peter Dunn, Australia @ War.*

Life was a 'boys-own' adventure for 'Jack'—Flight-Lieutenant Charles John Miles—and he was living it to the fullest. A boxer, pilot, and recently married man, Jack might have had it all, had it not been wartime, and if his occupation didn't require him to fly into dangerous zones. With the Royal Australian Air Force No.11 Squadron, Jack was no stranger to a challenge. He was tough; his boxing bouts had proven that, and he had faced danger in the air before that fateful day when Jack was authorised to proceed to Townsville for duty.

And Townsville was fast becoming a major staging point for South West Pacific battles; its proximity to Japan put the region in imminent danger. Before long, it was home to thousands of Australian and American troops... at one time Townsville was America's largest overseas air base except for some facilities in Great Britain.[1] Jack's squadron was amongst the throngs of military ready for action, and action came with the Japanese bombing of Townsville three times in July 1942.

If you couldn't find Jack and his squadron in the air, you could find them on the water.

Clipped wings

Jack's wings were a Catalina... named by the British after an island off California, and a most amazing plane. 'Cats' could stay in the air for up to twenty-four hours... so you can imagine, in wartime, a plane that can cross oceans and time zones could be most valuable.[2] When they wanted to come down, they landed on water. Catalinas were a unique rescue vessel too for picking up survivors in the sea; they were developed for these search and rescue missions. We (Australia) got our first one in 1941 (A24-1), and soon No. 11 and No. 20 Squadrons were equipped with more Cats as the growing threat of Japanese invasion began to be felt.[3]

Jack and three of his crew had previously taken part in an attack on Surabaya, leaving Cairns on 25 August 1943 for mine laying operations on the nights of 26-27 August 1943. In four Catalinas, the men attempted to close the harbour and trap the ships in the port.[4] It was a hair-raising raid. Luckily, despite seeing searchlights, they were not attacked. But when flying over Madura Island, Japanese soldiers fired at the four Cats; Jack's Catalina was "holed seven times by bullets and one of his gunners was hit in each leg by .30 calibre bullets."[5]

The Catalina of No. 11 or 20 Squadron in Bowen in 1943 beached for maintenance. Photo by Elliott Brand. Source: Australian War Memorial.

Bouts of boxing

Before he was fighting the Japanese and flying his Cat around North Queensland, Jack was in the ring; and he had made quite a name for himself. News reports tell of his many bouts including an amateur boxing tournament at Longreach, where the proceeds were in aid of the hospital and the officials were all well connected 'above' – the Reverend Hulton Sams was referee, Father Lane the timekeeper, and the Reverend Hicks managed the 10-seconds check (that is, alerting the time remaining in each round or the end of rest periods). Ladies were also present to watch the bantam-weight division fight, as Sandy Thompson and Jack slugged it out. The outcome was described by the *Huon Times*:

> *"Sandy Thompson and Jack Miles were both covered with blood at the end of the four terrific rounds. The referee, the Rev Hulton Sams, gave a decision, which was received with a good deal of boo-hooing. The rev. gentleman invited anyone who disagreed with his verdict to step into the ring with him. This quietened the gathering."*[6]

And Jack brought in the crowds. The *Daily Standard* wrote that Jack was an added attraction at the Metropolitan Amateur Boxing and Wrestling Championships at the Brisbane Stadium:

> *"The special interstate challenge contest between Ken Dainer, lightweight champion of New South Wales, and Queensland's most spectacular fighting machine, Jack Miles, is an added attraction for to-night's entertainment."*[7]

In 1931 when he took out the Queensland Amateur Welterweight title, Jack was hailed as our future boxing hope: "Good judges of boxing in Brisbane reckon Jack Miles... the most promising boy seen for years in this class."[8] Jack did go on to become the Australian Middleweight Champion.

Jack's boxing ambitions and Air Force commitments were managing to go hand-in-hand. On 30 August 1934, Jack was a feature on the circuit with *The Telegraph* writing: "The Queensland Amateur Boxing and Wrestling Championships will take place at the Brisbane Stadium. Jack Miles is now stationed at Townsville, and he is making the trip, and is keen to gain selection for the Australian team that will

Above: Jack in action. Photo kindly supplied by Janelle O'Brien (Jack's cousin), the Miles and O'Brien families.

tour New Zealand at the conclusion of the championships. The team will be selected immediately the championships are over."[9] Jack made the team and represented Australia in the Middleweight Championship against New Zealand at

Invercargill in October 1934. He was selected to go to the Olympics but they were cancelled due to WWII.[10]

Married and dispatched

In 1939, with WWII demanding Jack's commitment to duty, life became busier, but not too busy to notice Patricia Betty Mulder from Colac in Victoria.

When Jack turned 30 in 1943, he married 27-year-old Patricia. Patricia's father was also a military man (a private in the Australian Infantry Force), and it appears that Patricia was engaged in 1941 to William Frederick Borgeest,[11] but for reasons unknown (William appears to have been alive after the war, according to the census), Patricia fell for Jack, and they were married in May 1943.

In that very same year, Jack was sent on his final mission. It was in September when Jack arrived in Townsville for a travel flight as the Captain of Catalina A24-52, at the disposal of the Area Officer Commanding North Eastern Area, Air Commodore Arthur Henry Cobby (whom will later play a major role in this tale).[12] Jack was expected to be away for about four days and in the air for about 20 hours of that.

Patricia Mulder.
Source: Argus 1941.

A day for mourning

Just before 7am on 7 September 1943, Jack was captaining the Catalina A24-52 with 19 RAAF passengers and crew on board, when attempting to land in rough conditions, the Catalina crashed into Cleveland Bay.

Thirteen of the nineteen onboard were killed; Jack was one of them. The Court of Inquiry report[13] detailed the accident:

> "After touching down [on the water] the aircraft travelled a short distance and struck a large wave and sank by the bow. A film taken of the incident disclosed that after the aircraft crashed one or both depth charges blew up. The accident was considered to have been caused by a structural failure of the hull due to the aircraft alighting in a heavy sea. The aircraft appeared to have been serviceable prior to the commencement of the flight."[14]

The Catalina A24-52 accident, 7 September 1943; Jack was captaining with Number 11 Squadron. Source: National Archives of Australia.

Australia @ War noted: Divers later found that about 20 feet of the forward fuselage and one engine had been ripped from the aircraft when one of the aircraft's anti-submarine mines detonated during the rough landing."[15] The Court of Inquiry report[16] went on to say:

> *"Since a number of accidents have occurred to Catalinas at Townsville, it is felt that an order prohibiting the alighting of Catalinas at Townsville except in an emergency would be more reasonable and this is recommended in the recommendations of the Court."*

The George Medal

Remember Air Commodore Arthur Henry Cobby, who was the Area Officer Commanding North Eastern Area where Jack was sent? Air Commodore Cobby (1894-1955) had an impressive military career before and after his encounter with Jack. He fought in WWI, and as a result of shooting down 29 aircraft between February and September 1918, was described as "the leading A.F.C. ace"[17] and "awarded the Distinguished Flying Cross, two Bars to the D.F.C., the Distinguished Service Order, and was mentioned in dispatches."[18]

Air-Commodore Cobby. Photo: John Harrison, Australian War Memorial.

At the outbreak of WWII, he rejoined the RAAF in 1939, and Wing Commander Cobby took up the role of Air Officer Commanding Headquarters North-Eastern Area. He too was on the Catalina on that fateful day and was one of six survivors. The *Australian War Memorial* recalls:

> *"Air Commodore Cobby managed to extricate himself from the wreck and although injured, he re-entered the submerged hull on three occasions in order to rescue members of his staff. As a result of his strenuous efforts against the great pressure in the cabin he was able to assist Wing Commander W.L.B. Stephens, who had a badly broken arm, and brought him to the surface. The second time he extricated Wing Commander B.P.Macfarlan and brought him to a position on top of the blister. He re-entered the cabin a third time but was unable to effect any further rescues. Owing to the fact that at least one other depth charge was unexploded, and that at any moment the wrecked aircraft might slip under the water, Air Commodore Cobby displayed outstanding courage in risking his life while effecting the rescues of these members of his staff."*[19]

He was awarded the George Medal (for gallantry not in the face of the enemy).

Remembering the victims

Amongst the victims was Squadron Leader Leo Matthew Hogan – a local from Townsville. Leo, 43, was the son of Mr and Mrs M. J. Hogan, and husband of Constance Edna Marie Hogan. Leo rests in Section C, Grave A, Row 9.

Jack's parents received two telegrams: the first advised that their son was involved in a crash; the second advised of his death.[20] Jack's widowed bride, Patricia, eventually remarried seven years later, in 1950, to Michael Francis Considine. Jack's father, Arthur, died in 1957, Catherine (mother) died in 1975. Jack's siblings enjoyed a longer life than Jack: Tom died in 1965, Desmond in 1986; sister, Eileen, died in 2015, aged 86.[21]

After his death, the boxing community remembered Jack: "Flight Lieutenant C. J. (Jack) Miles, who lost his life recently was a former State amateur boxing champion and represented the State and Australia in competitions in Victoria and New Zealand."[22] To commemorate his life, Jack's mother, Catherine, and his younger brother, Tom, (two years Jack's junior) provided a special cup for an Air Training Corps Boxing Tournament in aid of Legacy at the Brisbane Stadium.

The newspaper reported: "Jack's mother, Mrs Catherine Miles, and brother, Tom Miles have donated the cup, which will be competed for annually. It is for the best performance of the tournament. There will be 23 bouts at the tournament."[23]

Jack fights on.

To pay your respects

A memorial on the Townsville Strand was dedicated on Sunday 14 August 2005 to remember this tragic event. Fittingly, it looks permanently out to sea.

You can find Lieutenant Jack Miles and his crew at Townsville War Cemetery as follows:[24]

Walk in from the side entrance and head to the north western subsection. Look for the eastern most row, and the 8th grave from the south, this is where Jack lies. Crew members can be found as follows:

- Flt/Lt Charles John 'Jack' Miles, (Pilot) – **C.A.8.**
- Flt/Lt William John Canterbury, (2nd Pilot) – **C.B.4**
- F/O Ronald Irvine Ferguson, (3rd Pilot) – **C.B.3.**
- F/O Gordon John Robert Hockey, Navigator – **C.B.2**
- F/O Reginald Albert Weeks – **C.A.16**
- F/Sgt Bernard Victor McInerney – **C.B.1**
- A/Cpl William Richard George Lobb – **C.A.14**
- Sqn/Ldr Leo Mathew Hogan (of Townsville)[25] – **C.A.9**
- F/O Charles Harry Ratcliffe, RAAF, Personal Assistant to Air Commodore Cobby – **C.A.10**
- A/Sqn/Ldr John Vernon Angus, RAAF – **C.A.13**
- F/Lt. Frank Haighton Lord, RAAF – **C.A.12**
- Flt/Lt William Archie Wilkinson, RAAF – **C.A.11**
- P/O Beresford Frederick Shearman, RAAF – **C.A.15.**

Townsville Catalina Memorial on the Strand.
Photo by Ian Bevege, reprinted thanks to Ian and Monument Australia.

Above: Jack in action. Photo kindly supplied by Janelle O'Brien (Jack's cousin), the Miles and O'Brien families. Below: Townsville War Cemetery layout map courtesy of The Commonwealth War Graves Foundation.

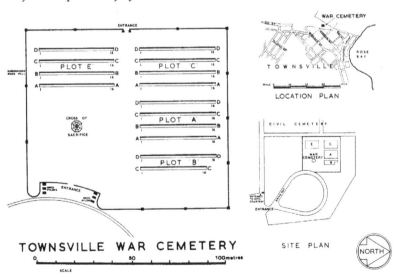

References:

1 Dunn, Peter, Townsville @ War, via *Australia @ War* 2015, www.ozatwar. com Retrieved 13 July 2018 from: https://www.ozatwar.com/tv@war.htm

2 McMillan, Andrew, *Catalina Dreaming*, Duffy & Snellgrove 2002.

3 Ibid.

4 Dunn, Peter, 7 September 1943 Crash of a Catalina at Townsville, QLD. *Australia @ War* 2015, www.ozatwar.com Retrieved 11 July 2018 from URL: https://www.ozatwar.com/ozcrashes/qld190.htm

5 Ibid.

6 PICKED PARS. (20 Jan 1912). *Huon Times* (Franklin, Tas: 1910-1933), p6. Retrieved 11 July 2018, from http://nla.gov.au/nla.news-article135822614

7 Boxing. AMATEUR TOURNEY TO-NIGHT. (1931, September 23). *Daily Standard* (Brisbane, Qld. : 1912 - 1936), p. 12. Retrieved July 11, 2018, from http://nla.gov.au/nla.news-article178957700

8 Round the World Boxing (9 Dec 1931). *Referee* (Sydney, NSW: 1886-1939), p16. Retrieved 11 July 2018 from http://nla.gov.au/nla.news-article136747779

9 Amateur Boxing and Wrestling (1934, August 30). *The Telegraph* (Bris, Qld: 1872-1947), p11 (City Final Last Minute News). Retrieved 11 July 2018, from http://nla.gov.au/nla.news-article181857727

10 McBrien, Jim, *From 'Ireland to Australia. A History of the descendants of the McBriens'*. 1st Edition February 2008.

11 Family Notices (29 Mar 1941). *The Argus (Melb, Vic: 1848-1957)*, p9. Retrieved 11 July 2018, from http://nla.gov.au/nla.news-article8151608

12 Dunn, Peter, 7 September 1943 Crash of a Catalina at Townsville. Op.cit.

13 - 14 National Archives of Australia: *Court of Inquiry on Catalina A24-52 accident at Townsville 7.9.1943*. NAA: A705, 32/17/143.

15 Dunn, Peter, 7 September 1943 Crash of a Catalina at Townsville. Op.cit.

16 National Archives of Australia: NAA: A705, 32/17/143. Op.cit.

17 & 18 Isaacs, Keith, 'Cobby, Arthur Henry (1894–1955)', *Australian Dictionary of Biography*, National Centre of Biography, ANU, 1981. Retrieved 11 July 2018 from: http://adb.anu.edu.au/biography/cobby-arthur-henry-5700/text9635

19 George Medal : Air Commodore A H Cobby, RAAF, *Australian War Memorial*. Retrieved 11 July 2018 from URL: https://www.awm.gov.au/collection/C960776

20 Dunn, Peter, 7 September 1943 Crash of a Catalina at Townsville. Op.cit.

21 O'Brien, Janelle, Eileen Mary Miles Ponsford, *Find a Grave*, 14 December 2017. Retrieved 11 July 2018 from URL: https://www.findagrave.com/memorial/185910662/eileen-mary-ponsford

22 PERSONAL (21 Sept 1943). *Townsville Daily Bulletin* (Qld: 1907-1954), p2. Retrieved 11 July 2018 from http://nla.gov.au/nla.news-article63149815

23 CALTAUX SAYS: HAS RIGHT PUNCH TO K.O. BURNS (1944, December 3). *Sunday Mail* (Brisbane, Qld.: 1926 - 1954), p. 7. Retrieved July 11, 2018, from http://nla.gov.au/nla.news-article97947368

24 Townsville War Cemetery grave locations courtesy of The *Commonwealth War Graves Foundation* (CWGF), 19 July 2018. Retrieved from URL: https://www.cwgc.org/

Images:

- On the wing of Catalina A24-49 on 6 May 1943. Photo from Ms Eileen Ponsford (Jack's sister, deceased). Reprinted with kind permission from Peter Dunn, *Australia @ War*: https://www.ozatwar.com/ozcrashes/qld190.htm

- Brand, Elliott [Photographer], Catalina (PBY) flying boat of No. 11 Squadron or No. 20 Squadron RAAF, early in 1943. Bowen, Qld. 1943. *Australian War Memorial*. Retrieved 11 July 2018 from URL: https://www.awm.gov.au/collection/P01490.002

- Jack, the boxer. Photos kindly supplied by Janelle O'Brien & the O'Brien and Miles families, and the latter as featured in *From Ireland to Australia. A History of the descendants of the McBriens* by Jim McBrien, Feb 2008.

- Patricia Mulder photo: Family Notices (1941, March 29). *The Argus* (Melb, Vic: 1848-1957), p9. Retrieved 19 July 2018 from: http://nla.gov.au/nla.news-article8151608

- From the collection of the National Archives of Australia. Accident - Catalina A24-52 - Number 11 Squadron - 7/9/1943 at Townsville. Series Number: A11083, NAA: A11083, 906/366/P1 PHOTO7, Item barcode: 4746414.

- Harrison, John Thomas [maker] Wing Commander Cobby, *Australian War Memorial*. Accession No. 000811, Victoria, Melbourne, Laverton, 20 February 1940. Retrieved 11 July 2018 from URL: https://www.awm.gov.au/collection/C23310

- Bevege, Ian [Photographer] Townsville Catalina Memorial, *Monument Australia*. Retrieved 19 July 2018 from URL: http://monumentaustralia.org.au/themes/conflict/ww2/display/100885-catalina-flying-boat-memorial/photo/1

- Townsville War Cemetery map courtesy of Commemorations and War Graves, the *Department of Veterans' Affairs* and *The Commonwealth War Graves Foundation*. Retrieved 19 July 2018 from: https://www.cwgc.org/

Pitman, Abraham [Photographer], Jack's grave, Townsville War Cemetery, 2018.

The Paronellas of Paronella Park

José and Margarita

Interred: José Paronella, 26 February 1887 – 23 August 1948 (aged 61 years*). Margarita Paronella, 1902 – 2 April 1967 (aged 65 years).

Location: José's and Margarita's graves were originally in Innisfail Cemetery, Section 14, Lot 9, Row 4. A marker can be seen on site. The original headstones *(pictured)* were moved to their home in Paronella Park.

Cemetery: Innisfail Cemetery, 8 Scullen Avenue, Mighell, QLD 4860

Original headstones: at Paronella Park, 1671 Japoonvale Road, Mena Creek, QLD 4871.

(*José's gravestone lists his age at death as 60, but his birth date is believed to be 26 February 1887[1] which would make him 61 at the time of his death).

Days spent cutting sugar cane must have seemed a long way from 25-year-old José Paronella's life as a baker in La Vall de Santa Creu – a small village in North East Catalonia, Spain.[2] But when he arrived in Australia in 1913—the youngest of six children striking out on his own—that's just what José did.

A young, ambitious José Paronella. Kindly supplied by the Evans family of Paronella Park.

It was while he was working in Pamplona that José saw an advertisement to work in Australia and having set sail from Genoa, José disembarked from the 'Seydlitz'[3] in Sydney on 24 July 1913, arriving to begin his new life.

To hear José's story makes you admire his perseverance. He heard there was work going in North Queensland cutting sugar cane, so José took a coastal steamer and headed north. He first tried working in the Cloncurry copper mines, but the heat and living conditions drove him away after four months, and he headed to the coast.[4] There he found other Spaniards and Italians, and plenty of work on the cane gangs in Innisfail. He blistered, ached, and is said to have hated every minute of the cane cutting season, and then he took on the role of a cook. But the traditional cooking that José served, including pasta and rice, was 'foreign food' to the meat-loving palate of local workers, proving yet another challenge.[5]

However, José put up with the derision about his accent, his cooking, his European ways, because he had a vision. He wasn't afraid of hard work, he had a mind for business, and he saved every shilling towards a piece of land that would give him security.[6] Over the next 11 years, he purchased a number of cane farms (as many as 12), improved methods and re-sold them.[7] Clearing, harvesting and eventually turning a profit from crops... a very good profit. Not far from his thoughts were the stories his grandmother told young José of castles, romance and drama.[8] One day, he'd have his own castle.

The wrong attention

On 5 October 1921, eight years after his arrival, José became an Australian citizen. With his new status of landowner and new-found wealth, he was attracting attention, and not all of it good. He became a target for 'The Black Hand' – a sinister organisation that preyed on the Italian cane workers in North Queensland. ABC journalist, Adam Grossetti[9] captures it well:

"Imagine you left your homeland and came here for a better life. A country in which you barely speak the language, where you might be resented for 'living on the smell of an oily rag' or taking job opportunities from others and treated as a third-class citizen. Then just as you start to make a few dollars—or even prosper— you're targeted by members of your own community and threatened with death if you don't pay extortion

demands. Returning to your country of birth is impossible. Going to the police is problematic; you don't know who to trust. This was the case for a section of the migrant Italian community in North Queensland when faced with a gang of their own countrymen calling themselves, La Mano Nera—the Black Hand."

José was now faced with paying up; but in order to avoid dire consequences from this, and the Australian tax department, José returned to Spain.[10]

A bride and a home-coming

In 1924 José went to honour his agreement to marry a woman in Spain, but while he was away, she had married someone else. Fortunately, the lady in question's sister, Margarita, was single and her hand in marriage was offered to restore the family's honour.[11] They wed on 16 September 1925; José was now 37, his new bride was 23.

And what a life change it would be for Margarita. While José talked of Spanish castles and creating a dream park, it is unlikely Margarita could have imagined the challenges of arriving in a new country, learning English, dealing with the heat and the terrifying spiders, snakes and all manner of wildlife. But like her husband, Margarita was stoic, and she supported his dream, all the way from Spain to Mena Creek in North Queensland.

The Paronellas returned to Australia and José had his sights set on 13 acres up for sale… virgin scrub along Mena Creek. For the princely sum of 120 pounds, José bought the land in 1929[12] and this land we would come to know as Paronella Park.

José and Margarita's wedding photo. Kindly supplied by the Evans family of Paronella Park.

Paronella Park is born

His vision: pleasure gardens and a reception centre and the site was perfect for a Spanish castle. The land featured beautiful swimming areas, lush green gardens for the making and the perfect escape for the nearby town folk, especially from the canefields.

José began with a stone house for himself and Margarita (and their pending family – a daughter, Teresa and son, Joe). Then the vision began with the construction of the Grand Staircase... grand it was but initially it was constructed to move the river sand that was needed for concrete making. The concrete "was mixed in a machine made from a Model A Ford chassis, an old Mangle Washing Machine and a 44 Gallon Drum."[13] And every structure was made of concrete covered with plaster – their fingerprints embedded for posterity.[14]

It was a huge job and outlay of funds but José was a hard worker and shrewd business man, sourcing material from his own property and hiring inexpensive labour.[15] Upwards of 7000 trees were planted, and a tunnel was excavated through a small hill, bringing wanderers out to Teresa Falls, named after José and Margarita's daughter. The creek was lined with rocks and traversed by small bridges… little touches that would ensure guests were in touch with nature.

The park was not only José's vision but it was visionary: the Hydro Electric generating plant, commissioned in 1933, was the earliest in North Queensland, and supplied power to the entire Park.[16] They laboured with unswerving determination, until 1935, when Paronella Park—José and Margarita's blood, sweat and tears—was officially opened to the public. A 'review' in the 1936 *Townsville Bulletin* described it faithfully:

> *"A man joined partnership with Nature and built this lovely spot around Mena Creek Falls. What a vision of beauty he had, and how ably he has carried out that dream!"[17]*

And in the *Cairns Post* in the same year:

> *"Residents of Cairns and district are indeed very fortunate in having such a wonderland as Paronella Park at their door. This much sought after beauty spot, with its quaint buildings, beautiful jungle and delightful waterfall and natural swimming pool has been the, admiration of all southern visitors."[18]*

Above: Mena Creek Falls, Paronella Park, c.1935.
Below: Tea Tables at Mena Creek, Paronella Park c.1935.
Source: Queensland State Archives.

Above: José on the Paronella Park Grand Staircase, c.1935. Source: Qld State Archives. Below: José with park visitors in front of the Refreshment Rooms. Kindly supplied by the Evans family of Paronella Park.

A retreat for the community

José had created the perfect retreat: "The Theatre showed movies every Saturday night. In addition, with canvas chairs removed, the Hall was a favourite venue for dances and parties. A unique feature was the myriad reflector, a great ball covered with 1270 tiny mirrors, suspended from the ceiling."[19] There was the Paronella Museum, the Tea Gardens, and the swimming pool was extremely popular. Guests could meander along José's well-planned paths marked with planters, have a hit of tennis on either of the two courts, or take the children to the playground, The Meadow, situated near the creek. Paronella Park had something for everyone.

It must have been comforting for Margarita to enjoy social events with other Spanish residents, where she could comfortably speak her own language. The couple also conducted fund-raising events for the Spanish Civil War.[20]

During the 2nd World War, US troops in the area frequented Paronella Park, bringing their girlfriends to enjoy a swim, dining and dancing. They weren't short of a dollar and every Sunday, about 70 American troops would arrive; Margarita is said to have prepared paella for them with home-grown tomatoes and herbs – their tastes more accommodating than those of the local boys.[21]

A family business

As the children grew, they worked in the business. Teresa's musical skills were a drawcard especially during the war years. While her father played guitar and her brother Joe played piano (boogie-woogie genre)[22] privately, Teresa's piano playing was described as: "so popular with the homesick American servicemen that they helped her in the kitchen so she was able to finish work early and entertain the guests. Her repertoire consisted of popular tunes of the day; jazz, dance and old time."[23]

Eventually, when José and Margarita's children, Teresa and Joe, found partners and married, their partners worked in the business for some time too. Teresa married Pino Zerlotti (at Paronella Park, of course) and Joe married Valentina Ribes in 1952, and had two sons, Joe (José) and Kerry. They kept the business alive and the dream a reality. Valentina lived and worked at Paronella Park for 24 years, and Teresa's husband, Pino, taught people how to dance at the Park.[24] Teresa and her husband Pino eventually moved to Brisbane.

Health and the elements

At the end of WWII, José was not a well man. Unable to work and feeling ill, José's stress was no doubt exacerbated by the climate. North Queensland residents are no strangers to dealing with the elements and in 1946 the wet season introduced itself to José and his family with disastrous effects. The first rains pushed logs downstream into the creek, piling up against a railway bridge a few hundred metres from the Castle. Pressure built, water backed up and with a snap, the bridge broke and the water and logs descended on Paronella Park.

Devastated, José and Margarita surveyed the damage: "The downstairs Refreshment Rooms were all but destroyed, the Hydro was extensively damaged, as was the Theatre and Foyer."[25] Then, they began to rebuild.

Over the decades, nature continued to challenge Paronella

Park. In 1979, a fire swept through the Castle, closing it for a brief time; Cyclone Winifred in 1986; flooding in January 1994; Cyclone Larry in March 2006; and Cyclone Yasi in January 2011, but nothing stopped José's vision continuing.

What became of José, Margarita and Paronella Park?

José had been diagnosed with inoperable cancer of the stomach, and he died on 23 August 1948, aged 60, leaving Margarita, daughter Teresa, and son Joe, to carry on. A genuine love between husband and wife was expressed two years after José's death when Margarita ran this small piece in the *Cairns Post – In Memoriam*[26] section:

Two years have gone by
Since I last saw your smile;
There is not a moment that I can forget.
The sad day you passed away;
I have wonderful memories of you, dear Joe;
And wish you could be with me each day."

In 1967 Margarita died, aged 65. Her son Joe died in 1972, leaving his wife Val and the two boys to keep the Paronella vision alive. In 1993 Paronella Park was sold to Mark and Judy Evans, whose love for the Park and its surrounds sees it continue. In 2009 the original 1930s hydro electric system was restored and completed at a cost of $450,000, and again to this day, provides all of the Park's electricity requirements.

Paronella Park has won strings of awards for its contribution to tourism, heritage and Ecotourism and it gained National Trust listing in 1997. The Paronella name continues to contribute to the community of North Queensland – Jose's grandson, Joe Paronella, is the Mayor of the Tablelands Regional Council at the time of publishing this book. As for Paronella Park, many generations have marked occasions of their lives within the grounds, many have wandered through the Park, enjoyed the dramatic waterfall, the moss-covered Castle, the lushness of the grounds – José's legacy lives on.

Where to find José and Margarita's graves:

José's and Margarita's graves lie in Innisfail Cemetery about 25km from Paronella Park. Their original headstones were moved to Paronella Park and can be seen there, at their home, where their spirit no doubt rests. You can visit: www.paronellapark.com.au for directions.

Images:

Images kindly supplied by the Evans family of Paronella Park:

- José and Margarita's headstones at Paronella Park;
- José and Margarita's wedding day;
- A young, hard-working and ambitious José Paronella; and,
- José with park visitors in front of the Refreshment Rooms.

Mena Creek Falls, Paronella Park, c.1935, *Queensland State Archives,* Item ID1334, Photographic material. Retrieved 17 July 2018 from URL: http://www.archivessearch.qld.gov.au/Image/DigitalImageDetails. aspx?ImageId=1334

Tea Tables at Mena Creek, Paronella Park, c.1935, *Queensland State Archives,* ID1083875, Retrieved 17 July 2018 from:http://www.archivessearch.qld.gov.au/Image/DigitalImageDetails. aspx?ImageId=1338

José on the staircase at Paronella Park, c.1935, *Queensland State Archives,* Item ID 1083877, Photographic material. Retrieved 17 July 2018 from URL: http://www.archivessearch.qld.gov.au/Search/ItemDetails.aspx?ItemId=1083877

References:

1-3 *Catalan Footprint in Australia*, The Portrait: José Paronella. Retrieved 17 July 2018 from: http://www.catalanfootprintinaustralia.net/scr/art/?id=41

4   Miller, Simon, Queensland's Spanish castle, 26 July 2012, *State Library of Queensland*. Retrieved 17 July 2018 from URL: http://blogs.slq.qld.gov.au/jol/2012/07/26/queenslands-spanish-castle/

5 -6 *Catalan Footprint in Australia*. Op.cit.

7 History of Paronella Park, 2014. Retrieved 17 July 2018 from URL: http://www.paronellapark.com.au/about/brief-history

8 *Catalan Footprint in Australia*. Op.cit.

9 Grossetti, Adam, Unravelling an enigma: In search of the truth of North Queensland's Black Hand, *RN ABC,* Monday 9 May 2016. Retrieved 17 July 2018 from URL: http://www.abc.net.au/radionational/programs/earshot/in-search-of-the-truth-of-north-queenslands-black-hand-gang/7338764

10 -11 *Catalan Footprint in Australia,* Op.cit.

12 History of Paronella Park, 2014. Op.cit.

13 Tropical Coast Top Ten #9 - Paronella Park, *Tropical Coast Tropical North Queensland*, May 10, 2017. Retrieved 18 July 2018 from URL: https://www.tropicalcoasttourism.com.au/news/tropical-coast-top-ten-9-paronella-park/

14 History of Paronella Park, 2014. Op.cit.

15 *Catalan Footprint in Australia*. Op.cit.

16 History of Paronella Park, 2014. Op.cit.

17 PARONELLA PARK. (6 Oct 1936). *Townsville Daily Bulletin* (Qld: 1907-1954), p9. Retrieved 18 July 2018, from http://nla.gov.au/nla.news-article62774071

18 EXCURSIONS. (2 October 1936). *Cairns Post* (Qld.: 1909-1954), p3. Retrieved 18 July 2018 from http://nla.gov.au/nla.news-article41784028

19 History of Paronella Park, 2014. Op.cit.

20 -21 *Catalan Footprint in Australia*. Op.cit.

22 - 24 Mitchell, Anne, Paronella Park: Music, Migration and the 'Tropical Exotic', *Southern Cross University*. Retrieved 18 July 2018 from URL: https://journals.jcu.edu.au/etropic/article/download/3343/3283

25 History of Paronella Park, 2014. Op.cit.

26 Family Notices (23 August 1950). *Cairns Post (Qld: 1909-1954)*, p5. Retrieved 18 July 2018 from http://nla.gov.au/nla.news-article42679281

Tracks to the Tableland
Martin Brennan & Alexander Corbett

Interred: Martin Brennan, 1862 – 14 November 1887 (aged 25 est.).

Alexander Corbett, 1862* – 14 November 1887 (aged 25).

Location: Brennan: see notes at the end of the chapter. Corbett: ID 45554, Site 436, Map ref: d3, Burial #236 (see notes at the end of the chapter).

Cemetery: McLeod Street Pioneer Cemetery, 127-145. McLeod Street, Cairns, North QLD 4870.

I t's easy to understand why most people came to 'The Cape' – Cape York that is. They were driven by the word that caused more 19th century human traffic in this country than any other – gold!

Admittedly, the very first vision for the Cape was for a magnificent trading centre aimed at rivalling Singapore. The joint Queensland government/British enterprise was to have trading, maritime, military, as well as civil uses. It was called Somerset and lay about 15 kilometres from the very tip of the Cape. From 1864 to 1876, Somerset was the regional centre for Cape York. Despite the whole city being meticulously planned and some of it even laid out, the trading ships never came, and soon the government lost interest, and the jungle reclaimed what was planned to be a mega-port and trading centre as vibrant as Singapore.

And anyway, by now the Queensland government had gold in its sights. On the back of the spectacular 1867 finds at Gympie by James Nash—described in another story in this book—it encouraged wide-spread exploration not only by way of rewards for finding payable fields, but by commissioning exploration. In 1871 Charters Towers followed – said by some to be the richest goldfield in the state. The government must have wondered, would there be any end to this wealth?

Investigating the Cape

In 1872 The Hann brothers, Frank and William, were commissioned by the government to explore the Cape and reported finding traces of gold on the Palmer River. That was just the start. The following year seasoned prospector, James Venture Mulligan, confirmed the finds and that there were good rewards to be had... and the rush was on. Mulligan went on to publish his *Guide to the Palmer River and Normanby Goldfields* in 1875, but by then the best days on the Palmer were just about over.

But as a result of the Palmer strike, Cooktown literally sprang from nowhere. The Endeavour River had been the inlet where Cook beached his boat for repairs in 1770. In 1873 the settlement was founded at the river mouth as a supply port for the Palmer River rush. By the next year, there were 47 pubs in town. It was known as Cooks Town until 1 June 1874. Populations fluctuated as miners came and went, but it was estimated that by 1880 there were seven thousand people in the area and four thousand residents. The town had a railway line that was planned from Cooktown to Maytown but only made the 108 kilometres west to Laura before the gold was gone, and so was the government money for the track... 63 kilometres short of Maytown. The Palmer was the last of the great alluvial rushes.

Dispersing across the north

So, what happened to those who came for Palmer gold when the field went dry? They spread out around north Queensland, largely in the area between the two established ports – Cooktown in the north and Cardwell to the south. There was a little relief for the miners when James Mulligan discovered the Hodgkinson goldfield in 1876. It was not far from the town that would bear his name, Mount Mulligan, which in 1921 would see the worst mining disaster in the state's history, that killed 75 coal miners.

However the Hodgkinson gold didn't last long either. Some newspaper reports wrote it off as a total failure... others as largely a waste of time:

"The prospectors give no flattering description of the Hodgkinson as an alluvial gold field. It is patchy and extremely poor in places."[1]

There were 30,000 miners on the Hodgkinson at its peak. However, its decline was rapid, and by the middle of 1891, there were as few as 300.[2] There was little more alluvial gold after the Hodgkinson, and many of the miners switched their attention to tin mining in the Herberton area about 65 kilometres south-west of present-day Cairns, where Mulligan had discovered it on the Wild River in 1875.

The tin mining offered a chance to continue self-employment, and therefore independence, as alluvial gold mining had done. In the Herberton area those searching for tin and those actually mining it were spread out through the rainforest, and the tin, after a shaky start for many miners, was proving to be extremely viable. One report later said the Herberton tin-field was by far the most important source of lode tin in Australia.[3]

Transport and communication, or lack of them, were soon to come to the forefront in Herberton. As mines were established, materials and provisions needed to come in, and in order for the operations to be viable, ore needed to be processed and concentrated before being taken out to a port. Three new ports were officially opened up in this period:

Cairns in 1876, Port Douglas in 1877 and Geraldton—or Innisfail as we know it now—in 1879. The three towns also became local government centres and competed with each other, at times ferociously, for trade and custom.

But extra ports or not, there was still the matter of getting goods in and out. The terrain between Herberton and any of the ports consisted of a steep coastal range and dense jungle. Today we see vast tracts of sugarcane in these areas, with rainforest away in the distance on the ranges. In the 1880s there was no sugar cane, and the impenetrable jungle ran from the ranges down to the sea. There was no road infrastructure to speak of; tropical rain caused what tracks there were to become swampy bogs, and swollen rivers were uncrossable.

Rail to the rescue?

The 100 kilometres-or-so journey from Herberton to Port Douglas in these conditions was a nightmare, and in 1882, the seasonal torrential rain brought on a crisis in Herberton when supplies could not get up the track from Port Douglas. The Herberton miners were at risk of starving to death.

They called on the government to build a railway into the area to enable their inward supplies to be guaranteed and to ensure their profits continued by assuring the processed ore would get out. The question that arose from this was, of course, while the Herberton miners and business folk would get their railway… the politicians would see to that… where would the other end be located?

The decision would essentially be based on finding the most cost-effective way to negotiate the spars and valleys that lay in their way. To find a viable route over, around, through, or a combination of all three, of the rugged range that runs parallel with the coast from north of Port Douglas to the south of Mourilyan Harbour. These ports were two of the possible candidates – the third was Cairns.

The Queensland Premier, Sir Thomas McIlwraith, visited Herberton in December 1882 and was received like an old mate:

> "Sir Thomas was met about three miles out of town by a strong body of townsmen, consequently his entrance into Herberton had quite an imposing appearance, three buggies leading the way and about twenty horsemen riding in threes bringing up the rear of the procession. The railway question was very lightly touched upon, the route being still undecided, only that when all the necessary plans have been completed and the route finally decided upon we are promised that the work shall be proceeded with without delay, the money shall be forthcoming. The Premier resumed his seat amidst renewed cheering."[4]

Palmerston and his indigenous guides on the job

The government hired a man called Christie Palmerston to explore the possibilities and come up with the final route of the Herberton line. Palmerston was something of a character in his own right. His mother was reported to be Madame Carandini; a well know Italian singer... details of his paternity are not so clear.

His task, simply put, was gruelling. To give an idea of what lay in front of the construction workers, there is a monument to Palmerston and his teenage aboriginal guide, Pompo, in Main Street, Millaa Millaa, not far from the Palmerston Highway. It honours their battle with the conditions. Palmerston, Pompo and four other Aboriginals walked a potential route from Geraldton (Innisfail) to Herberton in 12 days. Part of the inscription on the monument says: *Palmerston had an exceptional ability not only to find his way through rainforest but also to work with rainforest Aborigines.*[5]

The Christie Palmerston and Pompo monument.
Photo by Diane Watson, for Monument Australia.

The labours of Palmerston were closely followed in the north – where his decisions would be a matter of 'life and death' for the coastal candidates – and in the southern press, including the *Brisbane Courier,* where his narratives almost gave him a 'boys own annual' image – he was definitely a larger than life figure:

> "*Came into open country again but after travelling three miles in this direction and seeing no spar worth surmounting, turned back; saw large number of natives some of who came quite close but did not molest me; shared all my matches with them and went on; they appeared very frightened of the dog; after returning Pompo went hunting, and was chased by a large mob of natives fully armed with spears; they came so close that he was obliged to use his rifle twice.*"[6]

Contestants' claims

Meanwhile, in the north, lobbying was continuing with each of the candidates advocating their town's virtues as the most suitable place for the rail terminus and port. Port Douglas believed it had an advantage because it was already the port through which goods came and went; Cairns argued that the sugar industry boom was grounds for locating the infrastructure there; and Geraldton (Innisfail) also based its claim on the strength of sugar.

Much had been made of Palmerston's trek from Geraldton (Innisfail) to Herberton, and that route appeared favourite in a close-run thing. However, when Palmerston's recommendation along with the drawings of George Monk, the government surveyor, went to Parliament, the Barron Valley route, in other words, Cairns, was the choice. On 16 September 1885, the *Brisbane Courier* reported:

"The House approved, after long debate, of the proposed railway from Cairns to Herberton by a majority of 33 to 5."

... apparently not such a close-run thing after all.[7] And so, on 10 May 1886, more than four years after their pleas for a railway line, the good folk of Herberton, had they been at the bottom of the range, would have seen work actually begin... well almost. The Premier of the day, Sir Samuel Griffith, turned the first sod in Cairns and the economic future of that town, Port Douglas and Geraldton (Innisfail) was decided.

Getting on with the job

The task now lay before those commissioned to undertake this complex job; construct a railway across a coastal plain, up the steep range and onto the tableland. The track builders would encounter dense jungle and escarpments with slopes of 45 degrees and drops of more than two hundred and fifty metres that were described as "literally death traps for railway workers."[8]

To complete this task would necessitate building 75 kilometres of track that would wind its way around 93 curves, through 15 tunnels totalling more than 1700 metres in length, and across 244 metres of steel bridges and nearly 1900 metres of bridges built of timber – and all this after shifting more than two million tonnes of overburden, rock and fill.[9]

Death and disease

The range railway would be a challenging mission even using today's equipment, but 19th century technology saw the workers limited to basic tools, some horsepower where it was safe, buckets, bare hands and dynamite. And to top all that off, for eight months of the year working conditions included tropical rain deluges, extremely high humidity and malarial mosquitoes – and for all of the year, Aborigines defending their territory.

Despite all those obvious difficulties that were to be faced by the contractors, it was a couple of avoidable matters that first cost them valuable time and money. The building of the line as far as Myola was divided into two parts; the first between Cairns and Redlynch… only a bit over 13 kilometres that was expected to be finished reasonably quickly because it was to be built over easy, level terrain. It incurred problems however, because it passed through swamps. The swamps apparently produced fevers which were either carried by mosquitoes or as a result of gases from the ground.

On 25 August 1886, the *Brisbane Courier* carried a most disconcerting story of the totally unnecessary death of two labourers… navvies. Doctor Samuel Hammond gave evidence at a hearing in the case of a man called William Bennet found dead from fever:

> "*Death was from exhaustion caused by fever and not having proper nourishment. The tent deceased was in was not a proper place for a man with fever to be lying in, or hardly for anyone without fever to be in;*

it is essential that a large tent should be erected on the ground, and some person appointed to attend to the men who were put in it when sick."[10]

Bennet had been ill for a week and died after not being given any treatment. The second man to die in similar circumstances—of fever and without treatment—was Thomas Holland. He was sent to the hospital but not given the required paperwork and was refused admission. Result: he died from lack of the necessary attention.[11]

And the absolutely terrible state in which some workers who fell ill from malarial fever were living was shown up by the case of a man called Hobson, who suffered without treatment at the railway camp for two weeks before he died. Henry Long, who was a wardsman at the Cairns hospital, gave evidence at the Magisterial Inquiry into Hobson's death. He said:

"*I examined the body of deceased and found a large bruise or bed sore at the bottom of his back, and at the bottom of the bruise there was a hole large enough to admit a man's little finger; the hole had been fly-blown and was swarming with small maggots; the deceased was covered from the knees to the shoulders with human excrement.*"[12]

Careless planning and inexperience

While conditions in the camps improved slightly after these inquiries, the whole issue of the contractor's responsibility for due care, and attention to his workers was a distraction that should never have arisen.

Building Stoney Creek Bridge for the Cairns to Kuranda railway, 1890.
Source: Queensland State Archives.

The second and rather bizarre set of circumstances which slowed progress, and eventually caused the contractor to walk away from the project, smacked of careless planning, inexperience or both. The steel rails for the track were manufactured in England and shipped to Cairns onboard the *Lowther Castle*. When the vessel arrived and attempted to tie up to the newly built wharf, it was unable to because the water was too shallow. The only way to get the rails ashore was on lighters (low open boats), an exercise that cost almost as much as getting them from England to Cairns aboard the *Lowther Castle*. [13]

This debacle not only delayed the building of both the first and second stages of the project, but pushed the work forward into the wet season which that year was huge, causing further delays and continued problems with malarial fever. A second company was given the role of finishing stage one… but it too, went broke. The job was finished off by the Queensland Railways Department and opened on 8 October 1887.

Meanwhile, work had begun on stage two from the bottom of the range to Myola, just past Kuranda, at the top. It was the toughest section of the job. As the clearing, filling, building and track laying advanced, so did the workers' accommodation and facilities. Navvies camps were transportable and having mushroomed at key points along the way, were dismantled and sprang up at the next. Some were precariously positioned on narrow ledges hundreds of metres above the valley floors. Some turned into mini-townships. The *Cairns Post* of 6 June 1888 painted the picture:

"The hitherto lonely bush is resonant with the sounds of labour, and several embryo townships are springing up

with mushroom-like rapidity. On the Bluff next beyond the Falls a camp of considerable dimensions has been formed during the last few weeks, comprising two boarding houses kept by Messrs. Shanley and Gray, respectively, the latter differing from the too frequent practice in that he employs a European instead of a Chinese cook. A mile further on is Mr. Rudd's head camp, where quite a canvas city has been called to life as by a fairy wand."[14]

At one stage there were 1500 mainly Irish and Italian workers on the job – and they didn't mind a drink. One of the temporary 'townships' had five hotels. And given the dangers and unpredictability of their existence on the mountainside, it was no wonder the navvies on this job were inclined to let off a little steam occasionally. There is no more dramatic illustration of the deadly unpredictability than in the story of the demise of Martin Brennan and Alexander Corbett.

Brennan and Corbett

Much of the early work on the second stage was done by trial and error... it was dangerous stuff. Particularly experimental was the building of the 15 tunnels along the line. The method used was to bore what was called a 'heading' which ran the whole length of the intended tunnel and then expanded into a tunnel by blasting. The tunnel was then enlarged to the desired size and the walls trimmed. The tunnel would then be timbered – that is lined by props and planking to stop cave-ins. Occasionally tunnels were timbered before they were fully completed because of the unstable nature of the rock.

Drilling the longest tunnel, No. 15 during the Cairns to Kuranda railway construction, c. 1890. Source: Queensland State Archives.

That may have been the case in tunnel number four where on Monday 14 November 1887, early on in the construction of the second stage, Martin Brennan and Alexander Corbett were amongst the men working at the Herberton end of the tunnel when apparently without warning, about 10 feet (3 metres) of the tunnel face collapsed under its own weight, even though it had been timbered. The *Cairns Post* reported:

> "*Two men were buried in the debris and instantaneously killed, their bodies when recovered being greatly crushed and mangled. The names of these unfortunate victims are Martin Brennan of Irish extraction, aged 40; and A. Corbett, native of Ross-shire, Scotland, aged 25. Both were single men. Brennan was employed as a ganger, and at the time of the accident was engaged in replacing the timber.*" (The *Cairns Post* later amended the age of Martin Brennan to 25.)

One other man was injured in the rockfall and a fourth had a lucky escape when his shirt was torn to shreds by the jagged rock, but he walked away unscathed.[15] It appears that Brennan and Corbett's employers and the Queensland Railway Department were prepared for such morbid eventualities and took the dead men's bodies to a hotel that plied its trade in one of the temporary towns, where coffins were already waiting.

Quite by coincidence, the railway line that ran out of Cairns township passed within metres of what was then the local cemetery... a useful coincidence indeed as the *Cairns Post* related:

"*They were detained there until the arrival of a special funeral train, which left Cairns yesterday afternoon at a quarter to one o'clock. This train, which comprised two composite carriages, a covered goods-van, and a brake-van, was arranged by the Railway Department to remain at the contractor's order until leaving Redlynch at half-past two on the return journey. A halt was made opposite the Cairns Cemetery, and the cortege, accompanied by the Rev. R. Newell and the Rev. Father Crane, proceeded to the last resting-place of the deceased, where the funeral service was conducted in a specially impressive manner*".[16]

We don't know much about Martin Brennan and Alexander Corbett. They may have been from Victoria or South Australia where the Herberton rail line contractor, John Robb, had carried out numbers of projects and often took his workers with him on to the next job.

We do know from the newspaper reports that 200 of their friends and workmates were present at their funerals. Martin may have lived or worked in Cooktown… or been part of the rush for Palmer River gold, as the priest who carried out his burial service was from Cooktown. Their funeral was attended by senior management on the rail project, and they were carried to their resting places by the gangers with whom they shared their strange existence, living and working on the range.[17]

To the onlooker the proceedings at the cemetery may have seemed strange, two funerals, one on the railway side of the cemetery and the other on completely opposite, courtesy of differing religious beliefs - Martin Brennan, son of Ireland, a Catholic, and Alexander Corbett, from the Scottish Highlands, a Methodist. But that onlooker would also have been, according to the *Cairns Post* of 16 November 1887:

> *"Much affected by the burial services rendered by the two pastors. The pall-bearers were comrades of the deceased, and this last sacred attention did much to enhance the solemnity of the occasion."*[18]

Later in the construction process, there were warnings about using local scrub timber as props or in the building of bridges as it would "snap like carrots". There was a suggestion that in the case of the accident that killed Martin Brennan and Alex Corbett, the timber propping up the ceiling in the tunnel where they were working "broke like fire tinder".[19]

The cemetery where Martin Brennan and Alexander Corbett lie is now known as the McLeod Street Pioneer Cemetery and details of where to find the two men are at the end of the story.

More lives lost

The railway construction went on to claim at least another 30 workers in accidents. Some fell from great heights to the valley floors below. One at least was killed while smoking near blasting powder and setting off a detonation. Another was killed when he got onto the wrong side of a log that was being rolled into a fire and was swept into the flames.

But while the project had its tragic moments, there was also the spectacular. In April 1890 when the iconic Stoney Creek Bridge, probably the most photographed in Australia, was almost completed the contractor, John Robb, invited the Queensland Governor to inspect the work.

Much to Sir Henry Wiley Norman's astonishment, Robb had ordered a full banquet with a marquee, tables of food and wine, to be served on the almost finished structure. The banquet, John Robb, the governor and his party were suspended many metres above Stoney Creek below with the waterfall cascading behind them. Hard to beat!

Quite a celebration in 1890 at the Stoney Creek Falls, bridge and viewing point. Source: State Library of Queensland.

The Cairns-Herberton rail line stands as a memorial to Martin Brennan, Alexander Corbett and the other men who lost their lives in its construction. It took until 1893 for the line to reach Mareeba and then another 17 years to arrive in Herberton... the place that nearly starved 28 years before.

The grand opening was held at the railway station, naturally, with the workers travelling to nearby Wondecla for a picnic... and the official party strolling to the Town Hall for what was described as a "more fancy get-together". [20]

After 28 years of waiting, it would want to be.

How to find Martin and Alexander in the Pioneer Cemetery:

Martin Brennan: The Pioneer Cemetery is in McLeod Street and Martin's grave is not hard to find. He is on the McLeod Street side of the cemetery directly opposite a building at 180 McLeod Street, which carries a banner on the verandah that says 'Herries House'. He is about 30 metres in from the McLeod Street fence and 90 metres or so from the Grove Street fence.

Alex Corbett: While Alex died in the same accident as Martin Brennan, he is buried on the other side of the cemetery – the railway line side. At the corner of the cemetery where Grove Street meets the railway line, you will find an entrance and a bitumen track that leads toward the centre of the graveyard. Follow this for about 50 metres and you will find Alex's grave off to the left, lying flat on some pine straw.

Take the journey: You can still travel on this remarkable railway structure up the range to Kuranda. You can find details on the Kuranda Scenic Railway webpage: www.ksr.com.au/

How to find McLeod Street Pioneer Cemetery:

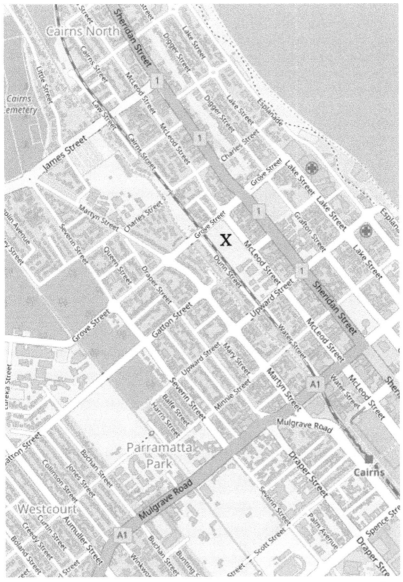

Map: ©*OpenStreetMap contributors.* www.openstreetmap.org/copyright

References:

1 THE HODGKINSON RIVER GOLD-FIELD. (1876, April 26). *The Argus (Melbourne, Vic. : 1848 - 1957)*, p. 6. Retrieved July 17, 2018, from http://nla.gov.au/nla.news-article7437711

2 MINERAL RESOURCES OF HERBERTON. (1891, July 27). *The Brisbane Courier (Qld. : 1864 - 1933)*, p. 3. Retrieved July 17, 2018, from http://nla.gov.au/nla.news-article3529117

3 Ibid.

4 Country News. (1882, December 16). *The Queenslander (Brisbane, Qld. : 1866 - 1939)*, p. 855. Retrieved July 20, 2018, from http://nla.gov.au/nla.news-article19788360

5 Christie Palmerston & Pompo, *Monument Australia*. Retrieved 25 July 2018 from URL: http://monumentaustralia.org.au/themes/people/display/91981-christie-palmerston-and-pompo

6 HERBERTON TO THE COAST. (1882, August 29). *The Brisbane Courier (Qld.: 1864 - 1933)*, p. 2 (The Brisbane Courier Supplement). Retrieved July 20, 2018, from http://nla.gov.au/nla.news-article3412357

7 The Brisbane Courier. (1885, September 16). *The Brisbane Courier (Qld. : 1864 - 1933)*, p. 4. Retrieved July 22, 2018, from http://nla.gov.au/nla.news-article3448686

8 Cairns Unlimited, *Kuranda Scenic Railway*. http://www.cairnsunlimited.com/kurandascenicrailway.htm

9 Nomination of the Cairns Kuranda Scenic Railway for recognition as a National Engineering Landmark Under the Australian Historic Engineering Plaquing Program, *Cairns Local Group of Engineers, Australia*, 7 July 2005. Retrieved 25 July 2018 from URL: https://www.engineersaustralia.org.au/portal/system/files/engineering-heritage-australia/nomination-title/Cairns-Kuranda_Nom.pdf

10 DEATH OF NAVVIES AT CAIRNS. (1886, August 25). *The Brisbane Courier (Qld. : 1864 - 1933)*, p. 2. Retrieved July 22, 2018, from http://nla.gov.au/nla.news-article4487056

11 Ibid.

12 Magisterial Inquiry. (1886, November 4). *Cairns Post (Qld. : 1884 - 1893)*, p. 2. Retrieved July 22, 2018, from http://nla.gov.au/nla.news-article39426407

13 Cairns. (1886, July 26). *The Telegraph (Brisbane, Qld. : 1872 - 1947)*, p. 2. Retrieved July 22, 2018, from http://nla.gov.au/nla.news-article174069500

14 Cairns-Herberton Railway. (1888, June 6). *Cairns Post (Qld. : 1884 - 1893)*, p. 2. Retrieved July 22, 2018, from http://nla.gov.au/nla.news-article39420336

15 Cairns-Herberton Railway. (16 Nov 1887). *Cairns Post (Qld.: 1884-1893)*, p2. Retrieved 23 July 2018, from http://nla.gov.au/nla.news-article39432031

16 Ibid.

17 Local Items. (16 Nov 1887). *Cairns Post (Qld.: 1884-1893)*, p.2. Retrieved 24 July 2018, from http://nla.gov.au/nla.news-article39432021

18 Ibid.

19 Alleged Sunday Trading. (1887, November 19). *The Week (Brisbane, Qld. : 1876 - 1934)*, p. 16. Retrieved July 23, 2018, from http://nla.gov.au/nla.news-article182631029

20 Atherton Herberton Historic Railway, *History.* Retrieved 25 July 2018 from URL: http://www.athrail.com/history.html

Images:

Watson, Diane [Photographer], Christie Palmerston & Pompo, *Monument Australia.* Kindly supplied. Viewed 25 July 2018 from URL: http://monumentaustralia.org.au/themes/people/display/91981-christie-palmerston-and-pompo

(1890). Building Stoney Creek Bridge for the Cairns to Kuranda Railway, 1890. *Queensland State Archives.* Retrieved 25 July 2018 from URL: https://trove.nla.gov.au/version/252849360

(1890). Drilling the longest tunnel, No. 15 during the Cairns to Kuranda railway construction, c 1890. *Queensland State Archives.* Retrieved 25 July 2018 from URL: https://trove.nla.gov.au/version/252849362

Unidentified (1890). Stoney Creek Falls, Bridge and viewing point. *John Oxley Library, State Library of Queensland.* Retrieved 25 July 2018 from URL: https://trove.nla.gov.au/version/167842251

Map: ©*OpenStreetMap contributors.* www.openstreetmap.org/copyright

Peter at his 'second' home, the Tobruk Memorial Pool in Cairns where his plaque (insert) can be seen. Photo kindly donated by Debbie Kurucz.

Barrier Reef Warrior
Peter Tibbs

Memorial:*   Peter Tibbs, 13 February 1942 – 1 May 2010 (aged 68 years).

Location: On display at Tobruk Memorial Swimming Pool, 370 Sheridan St, Cairns, North QLD 4870.

(Peter was cremated and his ashes remain in the care of his family).

It was to become a familiar scene in the crystal-clear waters at Green Island, 30 kilometres off the coast from Cairns. The casual observer would see a small dinghy bobbing in the mostly gentle but sometimes wind-blown Great Barrier Reef waters of the island's lagoon.

Upon closer inspection, the onlooker would observe two figures who would be visible for a moment, only to disappear over the side to continue the gargantuan task in which they were involved... a task so big it may never be completed.

It was October 1980, and since the late 70s, the Great Barrier Reef had been under attack from creatures that were, 20 years before that, just another one of the curious beasties that made up the population of the almost three thousand reefs that stretch for 2300 kilometres along the Queensland coast. And the two figures... Peter Tibbs and Debbie Kurucz.

Facing the threat

Scientific name, *Acanthaster planci*, but you probably know them as Crown of Thorns Starfish which have the capability of decimating coral reefs upon which they feed. What we now know is that they come in waves 15 to 17 years apart, but when they first showed up in numbers at Green Island in 1962, no-one knew how long they would be here and whether they would ever go away. All people saw at that time was a thorny, dinner plate sized starfish that crawled across reefs stripping them and leaving behind a white wasteland of dead coral.

There were voices that warned we would lose our reefs to this creature. Some scientists and tourist operators feared for the worst… Others told us there was nothing to worry about and the Crown of Thorns would stop coming.

Since 1962 there have been major outbreaks in 1978 to 1991, 1993 to 2005 and the present spate, which began in 2010. According to the Great Barrier Reef Marine Park Authority: *"The Australian Institute of Marine Science estimates the Great Barrier Reef has lost approximately half of its coral cover since 1985. The research attributed the loss to three main factors in the following order: cyclones, crown-of-thorns starfish and coral bleaching."* [1]

The reality of the situation was that in 1980, during the late 1970s outbreak, we didn't know what was going to happen… but we were learning… and it wasn't a pretty picture. The creatures are insidious and not to be underestimated. They are one of the few natural predators of coral and kill by pushing their stomachs out through their mouths onto the hard skeleton of the coral, eating the living tissue. An adult starfish can eat its own size in coral every night and consume 10 square metres a year.[2]

The insidious Crown of Thorns Starfish. Photo: Jon Hanson, Wikimedia.

With limited natural predators, there are plenty of Crown of Thorns Starfish. They spawn between October and February with large females capable of producing up to 65 million eggs during that time. In its early life it's not clear what predators it has, but as adults, its predators are said to be the giant triton snail, whose shell, unfortunately, is prized by collectors, the hump-head Maori wrasse, the starry pufferfish and the titan trigger fish. These are facts and figures that tell you that there doesn't have to be a big survival rate to end up with a large number of juveniles and adults.[3]

Moving north

Almost a decade before the great 1980s debate about Crown of Thorns Starfish erupted, a young man put his wife and three young boys in the car and left Townsville, where he was working as a teacher, to take up the lease at the Tobruk Memorial Pool in Cairns. His name was Peter Tibbs... a name the people of Cairns would come to know extremely well.

Peter was born in Warwick and eventually took up teaching. He worked in Ascot in Brisbane and Ipswich before heading to Townsville. In 1964 when he was 22, he married his wife Margaret and she was part of the adventure from that point on.

The school where he was the physical education teacher in Townsville had a broad teaching and swimming programme but it was particularly time-consuming for a man with a young family and so when the lease for Tobruk pool came up, Peter and Margaret jumped at it. They probably didn't have the faintest idea they would run it for close to 40 years... especially in the transient town that Cairns was in the early 70s.[4] It was on the hippy trail… a place where there were more lion tamers, trombone tuners and roof thatchers on the dole than anywhere else in the country.

By the time the late 70s invasion by the Crown of Thorns Starfish started at Green Island, Peter had opened his scuba diving business which would eventually become the biggest privately-owned dive school in Queensland, with shops on Green Island, Fitzroy Island and in Cairns itself. The attraction of diving was, naturally, the reef… the reef that was under threat from the starfish.

While he still ran the Cairns pool and in it trained some of the best swimmers the state produced, Peter was becoming aware that something had to be done to stop… or at very least slow down… the march of the Crown of Thorns Starfish.

Tackling it head-on

He was a determined man and he had his own agenda – at the top, getting rid of the marauding starfish. So, he did what he normally did when he saw a problem that needed fixing… he tackled it head on… not waiting for someone else to do something about it… not waiting for 'them' to fix it or the government to 'sort it out'.

While ways and means of controlling the wider spread of the starfish across the Great Barrier Reef were being investigated, most authorities believed the immediate control of outbreaks in small areas, such as around tourist sites, was desirable and that is where Peter started.

Green Island was continually one of the worst areas hit by Crown of Thorns Starfish. It was the first infected in 1962;

Peter en route to Green Island. Photo kindly donated by Debbie Kurucz.

it was where they first turned up again in the late 70s and it was where Peter had one of his dive shops. That was a good reason to start the fight against them there, but Peter was passionate about the reef and so anywhere the predators were was a good place to start.

Back then there were limited starfish control measures short of physically removing them from the coral, fencing off areas of the reef or injecting individual starfish with a chemical to kill them. Initially, the chemical used to kill the starfish by injecting wasn't available, fencing off parts of the reef was way too expensive, so Peter and his assistant, Debbie Kurucz, started taking them off the reef one by one with a wire hook on the end of a stick. It was painfully tedious work that consumed days at a time for very little result. The Crown of Thorns kept coming.

By the early 80s the chemical Copper Sulphate became available. It was the only known chemical that would eradicate them. These days similar programs use bile salts or common old household vinegar with considerable success.

But whatever they used, it was a mammoth task to inject each of thousands of starfish individually to clear a small area of reef which may have had a population of tens of thousands of the invaders. Again, Peter and Debbie spent days at a time floating above Green Island's reefs to kill off the starfish marching across them "like a swarm of grasshoppers."[5]

A thankless task

The *Canberra Times* and Brisbane-based Channel Nine Current Affairs Program, *Today Tonight*, both reported on the eradication program in which on one occasion during an eight-day blitz, Peter and Debbie cleared more than ten thousand starfish from the reef.

The *Canberra Times* painted the picture of Peter in his faded blue wetsuit on the beach at Green Island, squinting as he looked out over the area of the reef they had just cleared. What the paper couldn't tell was what he felt when he told the reporter that the starfish would overrun the area he and Debbie had taken eight days to clear in just two or three days.[6]

As the programme against the starfish continued, Peter tried different ways to keep the coral alive and healthy on the Green Island reefs. In 1984 he transplanted about two hundred colonies of hard coral from Arlington Reef, 11 kilometres away, to reefs on the northern side of the island's jetty. It increased the hard-coral growth slightly and introduced branching coral strains to the area, which may have offered better resistance to the creeping predators.[7]

The fight against the coral-consuming starfish is still continuing across the length and breadth of the Great Barrier Reef upon which the state is reliant for the tourist dollars it attracts. The Great Barrier Reef Marine Park Authority says there is a new outbreak happening at the time of the writing of this book and:

> "The primary objective for management and research in 2014–2017 is to preserve coral cover and to learn as much as we can from the current outbreak by testing improved methods for detection and manual control. Efforts will focus on reefs of high-ecological value, crown-of-thorns starfish 'spreader reefs' and prime tourism sites."[8]

Peter and Debbie (pictured) manually injected each Crown of Thorns Starfish with copper sulphate. Photo kindly donated by Debbie Kurucz.

Peter Tibbs, and others like him, in many ways led the practical fight against the Crown of Thorns Starfish and it is to their great credit that the battle against the predator is continuing so that: *"Protecting the Reef's heritage will help ensure it can be enjoyed by future generations."*[9]

Instilling ideals

But the people of the north will remember Peter Tibbs for many more reasons... reasons much closer to home, because hundreds of them... possibly thousands... learned to swim at the Tobruk Pool under the ever-watchful eye of Peter Tibbs. He said in an *ABC* interview:

> *"We've got people here now bringing what are the grandchildren of some of the kids who trained here in the first instance, it's been very, very good to watch how swimming can light kids up, how it can turn ordinary kids into people who have definite aims and goals and can transfer that into life after swimming as business people, or career people. They learn very clearly in swimming that if you sacrifice, you can gain rewards and it's a very good lesson to learn."[10]*

Amongst those he taught, and trained, was a young man who would go on to set new records in the north, but more than that, would credit Peter with being the man who made some of his goals possible– one of which was to swim the English Channel one day. The kid's name was Eddie Lovelock... and he had that dream when he was barely a teenager.

When Peter first saw him, he wasn't impressed and said in an *ABC* interview:

> *"He was a lovely little kid but he was no good as a swimmer... he wasn't a good sprinter which is what swimming's all about in normal terms."[11]*

In his fairly forthright way, Peter said he thought Eddie was lazy because whenever he took the young man's pulse after a long-distance swim it would be normal where other swimmers' pulses would be racing.

Green Island records

As it turned out, that was just the way it was with Eddie, and he blossomed into a fine long-distance specialist. And he still wanted to swim the English Channel. Peter said if Eddie could swim to Green Island, they would talk about tackling the English Channel. It was a deal. Eddie said he would do it to raise money for a blind classmate of his who needed a new braille machine.

So training for the Green Island swim began, and Peter devised a special regimen:

> *"We couldn't train Eddie with the rest of the squad when he was trying for Green Island because he needed greater distances. For example, we would get him in the pool later in the day, say at nine o'clock and we'd say: 'Eddie, your training schedule is 20 miles' and he'd do it. We'd often have him swim through the whole day, mix up a mixture of Sustagen and honey and a few other things and we'd let him suck that out of a tube while we walked along the pool. He'd swim on his back for a while and he'd suck down some food for lunch and then he'd keep on training."[12]*

The distance from the Green Island Jetty to what was the Cairns Marlin Jetty is slightly over 27 kilometres. Because of the current, Eddie decided to go Green Island to Cairns. The plaque to Eddie that is at the Tobruk pool says that on 18 November 1977 Eddie completed the swim without any assistance or the use of flippers in eight hours 33 minutes and 10 seconds. He had just turned 14.

Not long after he turned 15, Eddie made the swim in the other direction. Locals told him that he wouldn't be able to do it as the current would force him too far out to sea. Eddie didn't mind. He not only made the swim but did it in a quicker time than the first one: seven hours and 34 minutes. And he raised the money for his mate's braille machine.

On the basis of the two Green Island swims, an appeal was started to raise money to get Eddie to the English Channel for his shot at the big one. But sinus problems, which had plagued him for years, became worse and it just wasn't possible to manage a swim of that difficulty. The money raised was donated to a local charity and Eddie got on with life, eventually raising a family and running his business.

Four years later, at the age of 27, Eddie was diagnosed with terminal cancer. As his treatment became more consistent, he and his wife and three children moved down to Brisbane. He fought it for four years but died in 1995 at the age of 32.

The plaque to Eddie Lovelock that commemorates his life and his swims can be found at the Tobruk Memorial Pool in Sheridan Street, Cairns.

Hanging up his goggles

In his *ABC* interview in 2009, Peter Tibbs said that when the lease to the pool expired in 2013, he would give it away... retire. He and Margaret would have run the pool then for

42 years. His hope at that point was a simple one: *"We'd like to enjoy those last few years with the people who enjoy swimming here with us."* [13]

But it wasn't to be. Peter Tibbs died from cancer on 1 May 2010 and was cremated. On the day of his funeral, Peter's son, Rod, was asked why he thought his Dad was such a good teacher. He replied: *"We thought he had some sort of magic in him... but he denied that."* [14]

He may have denied it but there are plenty of people, including Eddie Lovelock and anyone who encountered Peter Tibbs, who would beg to disagree.

The memorial for Peter Tibbs is at the Tobruk Memorial Pool at 370 Sheridan Street in Cairns (see photo page 258).

Eddie Lovelock's plaque at the Tobruk Memorial Pool, Cairns. Courtesy of photographer John Huth and Monuments Australia.

How to find Tobruk Memorial Pool at 370 Sheridan Street, Cairns (marked with an X) where you will find Peter and Eddies' plaques:

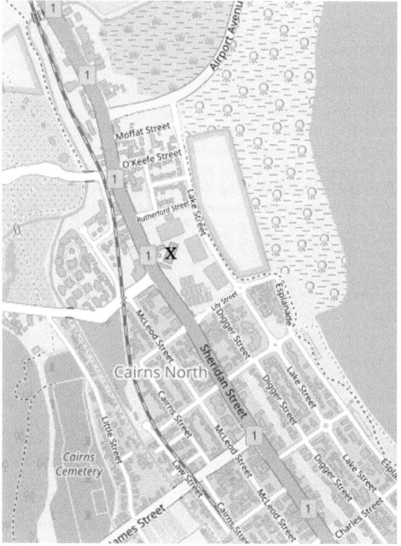

Map: ©OpenStreetMap contributors. www.openstreetmap.org/copyright

References:

1 History of crown-of-thorns outbreaks on the Great Barrier Reef, *Great Barrier Reef Marine Park Authority,* Australian Government. Retrieved online 29 July 2018 from URL: ,http://www.gbrmpa.gov.au/about-the-reef/animals/crown-of-thorns-starfish/history -of-outbreaks

2 Crowned predator reigns on reef. (News Review). (2012-10-06). In *The Sydney Morning Herald (Sydney, Australia).*

3 History of crown-of-thorns outbreaks. Op.cit.

4 Davis, Sam, A lovely way of life: Peter Tibbs, *ABC Far North Queensland,* 12 August, 2009. Retrieved 29 July 2018 from URL: http://www.abc.net.au/local/stories/2009/08/12/2654009.htm

5 & 6. 10,000 starfish killed by divers (1980, October 6). *The Canberra Times (ACT: 1926 - 1995),* p. 3. Retrieved July 27, 2018, from http://nla.gov.au/nla.news-article125625880

7 Baxter, I.N, Green Island Information Review, 1990, *Great Barrier Reef Marine Park Authority.* Retrieved 29 July 2018 from URL: http://hdl.handle.net/11017/228

8 What is the long-term strategy? *Great Barrier Reef Marine Park Authority,* Aust Govt. Retrieved 29 July 2018 from: http://www.gbrmpa.gov.au/about-the-reef/animals/crown-of-thorns-starfish/what-is-the-long-term-strategy

9 Heritage, *Great Barrier Reef Marine Park Authority*, Aust Govt. Retrieved 29 July 12018 from: http://www.gbrmpa.gov.au/about-the-reef/heritage

10 - 14 Davis, Sam, *ABC Far North Queensland.* Op.cit.

Images:

- The dedication plaque to Peter Tibbs at the Tobruk Memorial Pool, Cairns. Courtesy of Tobruk Memorial Pool, Cairns.

- Hanson, Jon [Photographer], Crown of Thorns, CC BY-SA 2.0 via *Wikimedia Commons.* Retrieved 29 July 2018 from URL: https://creativecommons.org/licenses/by-sa/2.0)],

- Peter en route to Green Island to undertake his Crown of Thorns eradication. Photo kindly donated by Debbie Kurucz.

- Peter and Debbie manually injected each Crown of Thorns Starfish. Photo kindly donated by Debbie Kurucz.

- Huth, John [Photographer] Eddie Lovelock's plaque at Tobruk Memorial Pool. Courtesy of John Huth and *Monuments Australia.*

Maps: ©*OpenStreetMap contributors.* www.openstreetmap.org/copyright

The diarist
Mary Beatrice Watson

Interred: Mary Beatrice Phillips Watson, 1858 – October 1881 (aged 23 years*). Thomas Ferrier Watson, 3 June 1881 – October 1881 (aged 4 months).

Location: Section: Anglican, Memorial ID: 61122088.

Cemetery: Cooktown General Cemetery, Charlotte Street, Cooktown, QLD 4895.

(*In some reports, Mary's birth year is listed as 1860 and age at death 21 years).

Portrait of Mary Beatrice Watson by Louis Buderus.
Source: John Oxley Library, State Library of Queensland.

W ords penned in a personal diary have throughout the centuries given us a front row seat at historical events; often the writer unaware that their musings would tell of a time, a place, or their own demise.

Teenager, Anne Frank, tells us in her diary entry written 20 June 1942, what it was like to be Jewish in Nazi-occupied Germany: "Our freedom was severely restricted: Jews were required to wear a yellow star... turn in their bicycles.... do their shopping between 3 and 5 P.M... forbidden to be out on the streets between 8 P.M. and 6 A.M...."[1]

Captain Robert Falcon Scott's last journal entry on 29 March 1912 before his death on a South Pole expedition reflects his resoluteness: "We took risks, we knew we took them; things have come out against us, and therefore we have no cause for complaint, but bow to the will of Providence, determined still to do our best to the last."[2]

The January 1796 journal entry of author, Charlotte Bronte, reflects 18th century society when love wasn't enough to secure a marriage: "I can barely wrap my head around the truth that he is gone and I shall never see him again. O how I loathe the way our society dictates our lives... love should not flow from the pocket but yet from the heart."[3]

And our subject Mary Watson's last diary entry on 12 October 1881 reads: "No water. Nearly dead with thirst."[4]

We know a lot about the last days of 23-year-old Mary's life because she kept a diary – a record of her desperation as she floated at sea with her baby in her arms. But how did Mary end up thirsty, abandoned and forced to flee her home?

Marriage, a baby, a new life

It was a life strangely off course for Cornish girl, Mary Beatrice Phillips. Hailing from her homeland with its continuous coastlines, sunny days and dramatic scenery (think *Poldark* settings), Mary and her family arrived in Queensland to start anew after financial trouble had overtaken her father.[5] Here Mary, a well-educated young woman, left her family to work as a governess to a businessman in Cooktown. She was 18, and after arriving, found the businessman, Frenchman, Monsieur Charles Bouel to be the owner of a night venue called Café De Paris[6] – picture the Moulin Rouge and a local Cooktown pub merged. When not acting as a governess, Mary played piano some nights in the Café, and it was here that she met her husband.

At 21 years of age, Mary married Scotsman and beche-de-mer (or sea cucumber) fisher, Robert Watson; he was 20 years her senior.[7] For the unfamiliar, beche-de-mer is one of the oldest fisheries in Queensland. Commercial harvesting began in the early 1800s catching species such as sandfish and selling predominantly to Asia for medicine and food.[8] So the industry was well established when Mary married Robert in 1880.

Mary promptly left the Monsieur and his business and moved with her husband, Robert, to the fishery headquarters on Lizard Island where Robert worked with his business partner, Captain Fuller. It was a new home for Mary, and an old home to the Dingaal Aboriginal people who had lived in this area for tens of thousands of years and considered it a sacred place.[9] It was also home to several Chinese and South Sea Islander workers, but no women or Europeans.[10]

It wasn't an easy life for Mary, in a somewhat foreign and

isolated environment, or with Robert, as extracts from her diary reveal in their second year of marriage:

25 January 1881: "Bob slightly annoyed – did not hear me answer him about putting an egg under a sitting hen. Both very silent."

2 February: "Bob and self great row… self half mad. All about my not answering him when spoken to."

24 February: "Bob and self great row again. I did not make any answer when he said something about the weather."

25 February: "Both very silent."[11]

Today, what remains of Mary's home on Lizard Island. Inset: the view from Mary's home. Source: National Archives of Australia.

When Mary fell pregnant she returned to Cooktown in preparation for the birth; Robert rented her a cottage where she remained until 3 June 1881, when Thomas Ferrier Watson, to be known as Ferrier, was born.[12]

It must have been a great comfort to Mary to have a child to care for and a family of her own at last.[13] A few weeks later, Mary and Ferrier returned to Lizard Island with Robert.

Mary kept up her diary correspondence noting the weather, and the fortunes of the fishing business, which was not doing well. As a result, when Ferrier was but four months old, Robert departed Lizard Island to inspect another possible venue for a fishing station. Mary was left in charge, assisted by two Chinamen, Ah Sam and Ah Leong.

Lives threatened

On Thursday 20 October 1881, eight or so canoes were hauled up the beach by about 40 Aboriginals returning to Lizard Island.[14] Mary was on sacred ground; not that the young Englishwoman had any idea of this or its consequences.

What happened that drove Mary, Ferrier and Ah Sam to set to sea in a tiny sea cucumber tank is not truly known, but an indigenous elder recalled several decades later (he was 10 at the time of the incident): "Ah Leong was confronted by the indigenous group while he was planting sweet potatoes. He was speared and killed instantly. The group then saw Ah Sam carrying water buckets and speared him multiple times. Wounded, Ah Sam ran for the shelter of Mary's island hut."[15] Mary's diary reads:[16]

September 30: Natives down on the beach at 7 p.m. Fired off rifle and revolver, and they went away.

October 1: Natives (four) speared Ah Sam; four places in the right side, and three on the shoulder. Got three spears from the natives. Saw ten men altogether.

Mary had to get herself, her son, and Ah Sam away from the island; no doubt saving her son was her priority. Mary and Ah Sam grabbed what they could—baby clothing, tins of preserved milk and other foods— and with no boat for their use, Ah Sam and Mary clutching Ferrier, pushed out to sea in a square iron ship's tank that was once used as a boiler for the beche-de-mer.[17] It was 1250mm (49 inches) deep and 1300mm (51 inches) wide.[18] Exchanging the peril that faced them on the land for navigating the sea… it was an act of desperation.

For just a brief moment, Mary must have breathed a sigh of relief; she was safe, off the island with baby, Ferrier, and Ah Sam. But Mary's diary covering the period at sea, 2 – 12 October 1881, tells of the panic and despair of the 10 days that followed.

Diary recollections

Their hopes of seeing a ship, being rescued or finding land came and went; they paddled and drifted, using Ferrier's blanket to signal if any ship came in sight. On a couple of the occasions they went ashore but were unable to find fresh water or were fearful of natives camped there and returned to their tank. Given Mary took some milk provisions with her, it is unknown if she was still breastfeeding, but dehydration would result in headaches and lethargy, and eventually Ferrier's milk supply would be affected.

What we do know are the events of her last ten days thanks to Mary's diary note extracts as follow:[19]

Left Lizard Island, October 2nd (Sunday afternoon) in tank. Got about three miles or four from the Lizards.

October 4: Made for the sandbank off the Lizards, but could not reach it. Got on a reef.

October 5: Remained on the reef all day on the look-out for a boat, but saw none.

October 6: Very calm morning. Able to pull the tank up to an island with three small mountains on it. Ah Sam went ashore to try and get water, as ours was done. There were natives camped there, so we were afraid to go far away. Anchored under the mangroves; got on the reef. Very calm.

October 7: Made for another island four or five miles from the one spoken of yesterday. Ashore, but could not find any water. Cooked some rice and clam-fish. Stayed here all night. Saw a steamer bound north. Hoisted Ferrier's white and pink wrap, but did not answer us.

October 8: Went down to a kind of little lake on the same island (this done last night). Remained here all day looking out for a boat; but did not see any. Very cold night; blowing very hard. No water.

October 9: Brought the tank ashore as far as possible with this morning's tide. Made camp all day under the trees. Blowing very hard. No water. Gave Ferrier a dip in the sea; he is showing signs of thirst, and I took a dip myself. Ah Sam and self very parched with thirst. Ferrier is showing symptoms.

October 10: Ferrier very bad with inflammation; very much alarmed. No fresh water, and no more milk, but condensed. Self very weak; really thought I would have died last night (Sunday).

October 11: Still all alive. Ferrier very much better this morning, self feeling very weak. I think it will rain to-day; clouds very heavy; wind not quite so hard.

And Mary's final entry on October 12 when she was alone with baby, Ferrier; Ah Sam preparing to meet his fate:

No rain. Morning fine weather. Ah Sam preparing to die. Have not seen him since 9. Ferrier more cheerful. Self not feeling at all well. Have not seen any boat of any description. No water. Nearly dead with thirst.

An agonising death by dehydration it can be; the constant distraction of being thirsty with a swollen tongue, feeling dizzy, faint, cramping, and having trouble sitting and standing.[20] Mary and Ah Sam were not only dealing with this, while surrounded by undrinkable salt water, but Mary knew her baby was also suffering.

Behind on the island – swift retribution

When Robert Watson returned to Lizard Island he was met with a devasting scene; buildings were burnt, Ah Leong was murdered, and his wife, son, and Ah Sam were missing. Stories began to appear in the local newspapers embellishing the truth: bodies were cut up, thrown into the sea and in one account, eaten! Regardless of the cultural differences or finding the truth, punishment was severely meted out. News headlines screamed "Lizard Island Massacre" or "Lizard Island Tragedy". One such account in *The Sydney Morning Herald* on 8 December 1881 before Mary, Ferrier and Ah Sam were even found reads:[21]

> *"THE LIZARD ISLAND MASSACRE.*
> *H. M. Spitfire returned to Cooktown this morning, after having obtained complete evidence of the murder of Mrs. Watson and her child, and of the two Chinamen, at Lizard Island. Mrs. Watson defended herself courageously as long as possible, but was at length overpowered, brutally outraged, and then tomahawked. The body was thrown into deep water. Several tribes are implicated, and the murderers, who were discovered, were all severely punished."*

What evidence? What punishment? Reports indicate that the police and native troopers shot as many as 150 aboriginals in retaliation. It was later revealed none of them had been involved in the attack on Mary.[22] This sad tale is no doubt one of many reflecting the challenges of early colonial settlement and how ignorance of indigenous culture resulted in tragedy for both cultures. Another ill-informed report in *The Capricornia* on Saturday 26 November 1881 says: "The baby was saved but getting tired of its crying during the passage to the mainland, they killed it also."[23]

What became of Mary, Ferrier and Ah Sam

After navigating over 64 kilometres (40 miles) of ocean from their departure point at Lizard Island, the three seafarers died of dehydration. They were not found until almost three months later on 19 January 1882, when a young lad from the schooner, *Kate Kearney,* anchored near No. 5 Island of the Howick Group, returned on board terrified at finding a dead, white person.[24] The subsequent search found the remains of Ah Sam, alone, and close by, tragically, the tank lay half filled with rainwater and the remains of Mary with baby Ferrier in her arms.[25] Nearby lay her diary.

It was surmised that Ah Sam's lone death was to ensure: "that he might neither intrude on the privacy of his employer nor pain her with the sight of his sufferings… whatever his colour, Ah Sam had some idea of the instinctive chivalry which is the attribute of a gentleman."[26]

Telegrams were received by newspapers that reported: [27]

SYDNEY, Monday.

The schooner Kate Kearney has arrived at Brisbane. Captain Bremner reports that calling at the No. 5 Island of the Harwick group, he accidentally discovered three skeletons, which proved to be those of Mrs. Watson, her child, and a Chinaman. The bones of the mother and child were found in a half-iron tank, in which they escaped from Lizard Island. A revolver, full-cocked and loaded, was by their side, and also a box containing clothes, account-books, and a diary. The Chinaman was found under a tree with a loaded rifle. Death had evidently occurred through thirst.

Newspapers reported on the finding of the skeletons. Source: The Gundagai Times and Tumut, Adelong and Murrumbidgee District Advertiser, 1882.

A funeral for all three took place at Cooktown Cemetery on 29 January, and almost the entire population of Cooktown attended. The event was reported as such: "Many ladies and children accompanied the procession – one who had known the deceased intimately following close to the hearse. It was difficult to ascertain the exact number in the procession but they may be reasonably computed at 650... After the conclusion of the service the Fire Brigade, headed by the Band, marched back to the Town Hall and headed the Chinese procession which accompanied the remains of Ah Sam."[28]

Diarist optimism

Mary, like her fellow diarists provided an insight into her life, last days, and a true explanation of events. The diarist shared an optimism, rising above their circumstances. Before her death in a concentration camp Anne Frank wrote:[29]

"I don't think of all the misery but of the beauty that still remains."

Captain Scott wrote in his last entry on 29 March 1912:

"Had we lived, I should have had a tale to tell of the hardihood, endurance, and courage of my companions which would have stirred the heart of every Englishman."[30]

Charlotte Bronte reflected:

"But life is a battle: may we all be enabled to fight it well!"[31]

...and 'our' Mary, never dipped into remorse or self-pity, holding hope in her last few diary messages:

*"Ferrier very much better this morning...
I think it will rain to-day."*[32]

Finding Cooktown Cemetery and Mary and Ferrier's grave:

The Cooktown cemetery is in the main street, Charlotte Street (also marked as McIvor Road), but at the other end from the commercial area. To find Mary's grave enter the cemetery through the main front entrance and follow the well-worn track for about 50 metres until you come to another track that veers off between graves to the right. Follow it for another 50 metres or so and you will come to Mary's grave below a tall palm tree. If you have trouble finding it look for: the palm tree – there are only a few in the cemetery, and the second is to line up a yellow house that would have been behind you as you walked the track to the grave and a green shed off to the right. When these line up, you are very near the grave of Mrs. Watson and son, Ferrier.

Somewhat ironically, a monument erected in 1886 in Charlotte Street to the memory of Mary is a water fountain. The small tank is in storage in the Queensland Museum. It is currently in storage, not on display.

Map: ©OpenStreetMap contributors. www.openstreetmap.org/copyright

References:

1 Forbidden for Jews, *Anne Frank Guide,* 20 June 1942 extract from Anne Frank's diary. Retrieved 24 July 2018 from URL: http://www.annefrankguide. net/en-US/bronnenbank.asp?aid=26200

2 Robert Falcon Scott's Final Diary Entry 29 March 1912, *History.* Retrieved 24 July 2018 from URL: https://www.historychannel.com.au/this-day-in-history/robert-falcon-scotts-final-diary-entry/

3 Gregory, Kristen, *Jane Austen, The Woman Behind Pride and Prejudice,* 17 Nov 2010. Original journal entry 15 January 1796. Retrieved 24 July 2018 from URL: http://www.highpoint.edu/education/files/2014/09/Jane_Austin.pdf

4 A North Queensland Epic (23 Sept 1931). *Worker (Brisbane, Qld: 1890-1955),* p5. Retrieved 24 July 2018 from http://nla.gov.au/nla.news-article71178798

5 Trotter, H., *Mrs Watson, a Cooktown heroine: one of the saddest of all the sad tales of the sea,* Port Douglas and Mosman Record Company, Qld.: s.n., ca. 1891. Retrieved 24 July 2018 from URL:https://nla.gov.au/nla.obj-344334529/view?partId=nla.obj-344336231#page/n12/mode/1up

6 Dalton, Trent, Mary Watson & the tank: A young mother makes a desperate bid to save her infant son, *The Weekend Australian Magazine,* 16 December, 2017. Cited in magazine and retrieved 24/7/18 from URL:https://www.theaustralian.com.au/life/weekend-australian-magazine/mary-watson-the-sea-cucumber-tank/news-story/db1edb48c3f20cafe369345e5ac434c3

7 Dalton, Trent. Op.cit.

8 Fisheries Queensland, East Coast Bêche-de-mer Fishery, 2012. Retrieved 24 July 2018 from URL: https://www.daf.qld.gov.au/business-priorities/fisheries/monitoring-our-fisheries/commercial-fisheries/data-reports/sustainability-reporting/fishery-updates/east-coast-beche-de-mer-fishery

9 History, *Lizard Island, Great Barrier Reef.* Retrieved 24 July 2018 from URL: https://www.lizardisland.com.au/about/history

10 – 13 Dalton, Trent. Op.cit.

14 A NORTH QUEENSLAND EPIC (23 September 1931). Op.cit.

15 Dalton, Trent, Mary Watson & the tank: A young mother makes a desperate bid to save her infant son, *The Weekend Australian Magazine,* 16 December, 2017. Cited in magazine and retrieved 24/7/18 from URL: https://www.theaustralian.com.au/life/weekend-australian-magazine/mary-watson-the-sea-cucumber-tank/news-story/db1edb48c3f20cafe369345e5ac434c3

16 - 17 A NORTH QUEENSLAND EPIC (23 September 1931). Op.cit.

18 Queensland Historical Atlas, Mary Watson's tank, 1881, *Queensland Museum,* 2010. Retrieved 24 July 2018 from URL: http://www.qhatlas.com.au/resource/mary-watsons-tank-1881

19 A NORTH QUEENSLAND EPIC (23 September 1931). Op.cit.

20 Symptoms of Dehydration, *The Life Resources Charitable Trust,* 2011. Retrieved 24 July 2018 from URL: http://www.life.org.nz/euthanasia/abouteuthanasia/methods-of-euthanasia1

21 THE LIZARD ISLAND MASSACRE. (8 December 1881). *The Sydney Morning Herald (NSW: 1842- 954),* p5. Retrieved 24 July 2018, from http://nla.gov.au/nla.news-article13500762

22 Kieza, Grantlee, Sad tale of Lizard Island pioneer Mary Watson..., *The Sunday Mail* (Qld), 13 Nov 2016. Retrieved 24 July 2018 from:https://www.couriermail. com.au/news/opinion/sad-tale-of-lizard-island-pioneer-mary-watson-forced-to-sea-in-a-tub-after-spear-attack/news-story/58103ab847dc64be388cee1f3f9d744e
23 Local & General News. (26 Nov 1881). *The Capricornian (Rockhampton, Qld: 1875-1929)*, p10. Retrieved 24 July 2018 from http://nla.gov.au/nla.news-article67201186
24 A NORTH QUEENSLAND EPIC (23 September 1931). Op.cit.
25 Dalton, Trent. Op.cit.
26 Trotter, H. Op.cit.
27 OUR TELEGRAMS. (1882, January 24). *The Gundagai Times and Tumut, Adelong and Murrumbidgee District Advertiser (NSW: 1868-1931)*, p.3. Retrieved 24 July 2018,from http://nla.gov.au/nla.news-article123470156
28 Trotter, H. Op.cit.
29 Tscherry, Laura, Anne Frank: 10 beautiful quotes from The Diary of a Young Girl, *The Guardian*, 27 January 2015. Retrieved 24 July 2018 from: https://www.theguardian. com/childrens-books-site/2015/jan/27/the-greatest-anne-frank-quotes-ever
30 Robert Falcon Scott's Final Diary Entry 29 March 1912. Op.cit.
31 The Letters of Charlotte Brontë Quotes, Goodreads. Retrieved 24 July 2018 from: https://www.goodreads.com/work/quotes/2698375-the-letters-of-charlotte-bronte
32 A NORTH QUEENSLAND EPIC (23 September 1931). Op.cit.

Images:

Buderus, Louis *Portrait of Mary Beatrice Watson*. John Oxley Library, State Library of Queensland. Retrieved 13 January 2018 from URL: https://trove. nla.gov.au/version/47908773

Nicol, Bob [Photographer] 1973, Scenic - Queensland - A view from the site of Mary Beatrice Watson's home on Lizard Island, Great Barrier Reef, Qld, 1973 (A6180). From the collection of the *National Archives of Australia*.

OUR TELEGRAMS. (1882, January 24). *The Gundagai Times and Tumut, Adelong and Murrumbidgee District Advertiser (NSW: 1868 - 1931)*, p. 3. Retrieved July 24, 2018, from http://nla.gov.au/nla.news-article123470156

Map:©*OpenStreetMap contributors.www.openstreetmap.org/copyright*

Pictured below and on p279 (1973). Scenic - Queensland - The site and remains of Mary Beatrice Watson's home on Lizard Island, Qld, 1973 (A6180). From the collection of the *National Archives of Australia*.

Acknowledgements:

Our sincere thanks to the following people and resources who shared their time, wisdom and enthusiasm to assist us:

- The production of this book was supported by the Queensland Government through *Arts Queensland* – our special thanks to Alyssa McIntosh
- Shane Bowering, *Red Tape Busters*, for grant assistance
- Vicki McDonald, State Librarian/CEO, *State Library of Queensland*
- *Monuments Australia* administrators Kent Watson and Diane Watson, and contributors: Ian Bevege, John Huth
- Pauline O'Keeffe, *Cairns Historical Society*
- Maureen Scutts, Administration Officer, Cemeteries, *Rockhampton Regional Council*
- Eileen Dwane, *State Library of Qld*, for amazing support
- Lee, *Mackay Regional Council* media team
- Brendan, Sexton, *Innisfail Cemetery*
- Richard Hunt, Hon. Researcher, and Ilona Fekete of *Royal Historical Society of Queensland*
- Lisa Ryan and Geoff Barlow, *Gympie Regional Libraries.*
- Robyn Maconachie, *CityLibraries, Townsville*
- Trina Reading, Community Learning Services Librarian, *CityLibraries, Townsville*
- Hayden Walker, *Walker's Weather*, Bundaberg
- Don Braben for allowing us to reproduce his beautiful 'Queen of the Colonies' painting
- Damon Bickle for allowing us to reproduce the image of his Great Uncle, Sgt. Henry Buchanan, and his efforts to keep the memories alive. Visit: https://thefieldsofpozieres.com/
- Bridget Evans and the Evans family of Paronella Park

- Lesley Buckley, Cultural Planner - *Cairns Regional Council*
- Marilyn Jensen, *Wide Bays Hospitals Museum Society Inc.*
- Kelli Stidiford, Librarian *Capricornia CQ Collection Library*
- Glen Hall for generously sharing his research: *www.mackayhistory.org* and '*Have you seen the Old Mackay*' Facebook Page
- Sr Joanne Molloy, *Sisters of Mercy* Archivist
- Doug Petersen, author, *St Joseph's Orphanage Merara: Mackay Orphanage Bucasia –The Children's Story*
- Neridah Kaddatz, author, pending biography on Father Bacus
- Maureen Scutts, *Rockhampton Regional Council*
- John Fletcher, *Rockhampton Historical Society*
- Bob English for Catalina background information (Bob's father was a navigator with the 11 Squadron)
- Margaret and Rodney Tibbs, and Debbie Kurucz
- Amanda Sexton, Community Programs Officer, *Townsville City Council*
- *The National Library, the National Archives of Australia* and the *Australian War Memorial*
- Ebony from the Tobruk Memorial Pool, Cairns
- Jan Bartlett, Commemorations and War Graves, Department of Veterans' Affairs
- Janelle O'Brien, the O'Brien and Miles' family descendants
- And most importantly, Joanne James, our editor.

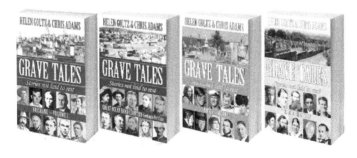

About the authors:

Helen Goltz: Helen is a journalist, author and producer with a 30-year history of working for newspapers, magazines, in marketing, and producing television and radio programs for clients including News Ltd, the Seven Network and Fairfax radio. She is the author of 12 books and is published by Atlas Productions and Clan Destine Press. Helen is postgraduate degree qualified with majors in Literature and Media.

Chris Adams: In his journalism career, Chris worked as News and Progam Director for Fairfax's 4BC; spent over 30 years in broadcast current affairs as a journalist and producer for Channel Nine's *Today Tonight* and Producer of Channel Seven's *State Affair;* reported as a War Correspondent in 1991 for the Persian Gulf War and the Civil War of Somalia in 1993, and is credited with over 40 documentaries.

Hastings Goltz-Adams: can sniff out a good bone (uh, story) from a mile away. He accompanies the authors where possible.

We would love to connect with you.

If you want to:

- find out where we will be appearing to discuss *Grave Tales* or to invite us to guest speak

- track us down on the road as we research our next book

- send us your photos if you visit our grave stories

- or share your fascinating grave stories with us

please connect with us via any of the methods below.

Website: www.gravetales.com.au

Facebook: www.facebook.com/gravetalesAUS/

Instagram: https://www.instagram.com/gravetales/

Email: enquiries@gravetales.com.au

Mail: PO Box 488, Stones Corner, QLD 4120

Lightning Source UK Ltd.
Milton Keynes UK
UKHW010015230819
348409UK00001B/78/P